APOSTLE

PAUL

The Life and Legacy of Apostle Paul
"The Journey of Faith

Dr. Maxwell Shimba

Shimba Publishing, LLC

TABLE OF CONTENTS

Biography of Apostle Paul v

Apostle Paul's Parents 1

Introduction 5

Setting the stage for the Significance of Apostle Paul 5

Chapter 1 8

Apostle Paul in the early Christian Movement 8

Chapter 02 24

Early Life in Tarsus 24

Chapter 03 37

Saul's Conversion on the Road to Damascus 37

Chapter 04 42

Theological Foundations 42

Chapter 05 50

Paul's First Missionary Journey 50

Chapter 06 58

The Jerusalem Council 58

Chapter 07 66

Second and Third Missionary Journeys 66

Chapter 08 75

The Epistles to the Thessalonians 75

Chapter 09 82

The Corinthian Correspondence 82

Chapter 10 94

Imprisonment and the Prison Epistles 94

Chapter 11 102

The Pastoral Epistles 102

Chapter 12 110

Paul's Arrest and Trial **110**

Chapter 13 ....**118**

The Journey to Rome **118**

Chapter 14 ....**125**

Final Imprisonment and Martyrdom **125**

Chapter 15 ....**131**

Legacy and Influence **131**

Conclusion **137**

BIOGRAPHY OF APOSTLE PAUL

Paul, an outstanding missionary, writer, and theologian of the early Church, holds a significant place in the New Testament and the history of Christianity. He authored 13 epistles, which constitute about one-fourth of the New Testament, and nearly 16 chapters of the book of Acts (13-28) are dedicated to his missionary endeavors.

Birth and Family Background

Historically known as Saul, Paul was born in the Asian city of Tarsus in Cilicia, as mentioned in Acts 22:3. This city is located on the present-day southern coast of Turkey and was one of the region's important cities. Paul was from the tribe of Benjamin and was named after the tribe's most notable figure, King Saul. His parents were devout Pharisees, deeply rooted in their Jewish heritage, and they were also Roman citizens. It is noteworthy that although Judea was part of the Roman Empire, most Jews were not granted Roman citizenship. Citizenship outside the Roman Empire was a privilege typically bestowed upon individuals who had made significant contributions to the Empire. It is widely speculated that Paul's father or grandfather earned this honor due to some distinguished service, suggesting that Paul's family was influential and possibly even moderately wealthy.

Rabbinic Training

At the age of fourteen Paul was sent to Jerusalem to be trained as a Rabbi (Acts 22:3) Paul was fortunate to have under studied a renowned, well-educated and prominent Rabbi known as Gamaliel. At that time Rabbis were taught another trade. The idea was to keep them from becoming a burden on society. They also wanted to have something to fall on during hard times. Paul was not an exception. He was trained to be a tent-maker.

Persecution of Christians

Paul grew to be a man of firm convictions and fiery personality. He always acted on his beliefs. Thus, when he was confronted with what he took to be a heresy to Judaism, he worked with all his might to quell it. This heresy would one day come to be known as Christianity and Paul was among the foremost of its persecutors. A very good example is when Stephen was being stoned. Paul was present. Although he did not participate, he encouraged the violent act that destroyed the first of the martyrs. He then participated in a general persecution including, "going from house to house, he dragged out the believers, both men and women and threw them into jail."

Paul's Conversion

Paul's conversion stands as one of the most dramatic and pivotal moments in the New Testament. Initially, he set out on a mission to Damascus, driven by a zealous determination to continue his persecution of Christians. His intent was to arrest those who belonged to "the Way," as the early Christian movement was known, and bring them back to Jerusalem in chains (Acts 9:1-2).

However, as Paul journeyed toward Damascus, his life was forever changed by a profound and miraculous encounter. According to the account in the book of Acts, Paul experienced a sudden and blinding light from heaven, causing him to fall to the ground. In this moment of divine intervention, Paul heard the voice of Jesus saying, "Saul, Saul, why do you persecute me?" (Acts 9:4). This question struck at the core of Paul's actions, confronting him with the realization that in persecuting Christians, he was, in fact, persecuting Christ Himself.

The voice of Jesus then commissioned Paul to be His chosen instrument to carry His name to the Gentiles, their kings, and the people of Israel (Acts 9:15). This encounter was not just a call to cease his persecution but a directive to become a preacher of the very faith he had sought to destroy. Blinded by the light, Paul was led by his companions into Damascus, where he spent three days without sight, neither eating nor drinking, in a state of deep reflection and repentance.

Before fully embracing this divine calling, Paul underwent a period of spiritual transformation. He spent time in Arabia, a region associated with deep contemplation and communion with God, before returning to Damascus (Galatians 1:17). This period likely allowed Paul to reconcile his past actions with his new faith, to meditate on the Scriptures with fresh eyes, and to prepare for the immense task ahead of him.

When Paul returned to Damascus, he began preaching the Gospel with fervor, proclaiming Jesus as the Son of God. His boldness in preaching confounded the Jews, who were astonished at the dramatic change in this former persecutor of Christians. Paul's message was powerful and persuasive, and it quickly drew the ire of those who opposed the new faith. As a result, a plot was hatched to kill him. Learning of this, Paul's followers helped him escape by lowering him in a basket through an opening in the city wall under the cover of night (Acts 9:23-25).

Paul's Dual Identity: Jew and Roman

Even after his conversion, Paul maintained that he was both a Jew and a Roman citizen. This dual identity played a significant role in his ministry. His Jewish heritage provided him with an in-depth understanding of the Scriptures, which he used to demonstrate that Jesus was the fulfillment of the Messianic prophecies. His Roman citizenship afforded him certain legal protections and privileges, enabling him to travel more freely across the Roman Empire and to appeal directly to Roman authorities when faced with persecution.

Paul's insistence on his Jewish identity is evident in his continued observance of Jewish customs and his deep love for his fellow Jews, even as he carried out his mission to the Gentiles. In his letter to the Romans, Paul expressed great sorrow and unceasing anguish for the people of Israel, wishing that he himself could be cursed and cut off from Christ if it would mean their salvation (Romans 9:1-3).

The Missionary Journey Begins

Paul's conversion marked the beginning of his lifelong mission to spread the Gospel. After escaping from Damascus, he traveled to Jerusalem, where he met with the apostles. Initially, they were wary of him, given his reputation as a fierce persecutor of Christians. However, Barnabas, a respected leader in the early Church, vouched for Paul, recounting his encounter with Christ and his bold preaching in Damascus (Acts 9:26-27).

From there, Paul's missionary work expanded as he traveled across the Roman Empire, establishing churches and preaching the message of Christ. His journeys took him to regions far and wide, including Asia Minor, Greece, and eventually Rome. Throughout his travels, Paul encountered various challenges, including imprisonment, beatings, and shipwrecks. Yet, his unwavering commitment to his divine calling and his profound love for the people he served propelled him forward.

Paul's letters, written to the churches he established, became foundational texts for Christian theology. They addressed theological questions, provided guidance on church organization and Christian living, and offered encouragement in the face of persecution. These letters, which form a significant portion of the New Testament, continue to influence Christian thought and practice to this day.

The Lasting Impact of Paul's Conversion

Paul's conversion is not just a story of personal transformation; it is a testament to the power of divine grace and the far-reaching impact of a single life dedicated to the service of God. Through Paul, the message of Jesus Christ spread beyond the confines of Jewish communities to the Gentile world, fulfilling the mission given to him on the road to Damascus. His writings and teachings have shaped Christian doctrine for centuries, and his life serves as an enduring example of faith, perseverance, and the transformative power of God's call.

Paul's Missionary Journey

He went to Jerusalem and there gained official sanction from the elders of the Church, including Peter and James, to bring the message of Jesus to the Gentiles. Along with Barnabas, he then went on his first Missionary Journey to Cyprus, Antioch in Pisidia, Iconium, Lystra and Derbe. During this journey they met many hardships. Paul was even stoned, though not killed, in Lystra. It was an ironic twist that Paul underwent the same gruesome punishment he had sanctioned for Stephen and for the very cause Stephen had suffered.

Around 50 A.D. he returned to Jerusalem to report to the church elders. His visit provoked a dispute over whether Christians had to first become Jews. Paul said no. The controversy was temporarily resolved in his favor and he went on his second and third missionary journeys to Galatia, Phrygia, Macedonia and Greece. He even went to Athens where he argued with philosophers as well as pagans.

It was during this period that he met Luke, a doctor who would become a close adherent and would eventually write one of the gospels as well as the book of Acts. After his third missionary journey, Paul returned to Jerusalem where he ran into a dispute with the Sanhedrin. He was the object of a huge civil disturbance. For this, he was arrested and eventually brought to Caesarea.

While there, he was questioned and tried several times, but his enemies could not seem to make their charges stick. Even so, he was held by the governor, Felix, who was afraid he might again create problems in Jerusalem. The next governor, Festus, seemed to be loath to come to a decision on his case, so after over two years of house arrest, Paul invoked his right as a Roman citizen to demand a trial before the Emperor.

He was sent on the next ship to Rome. However, the ship met heavy seas and wrecked on the Island of Malta. Paul prayed and was visited by an Angel and the entire crew was saved. Paul eventually took another boat and reached Italy. He was met by supporters and eventually made it to Rome.

Paul's final years

It is known that he spent at least two years under house arrest waiting his audience with Nero. Extant literature close to the time indicates that Paul was either tried or executed by the sword or he died during the persecution that came about after the great fire where Nero was reputed to have incited the blaze and to have fiddled during the conflagration in about 64 AD. Some tradition also has it that Paul escaped the persecution and went on to continue his preaching in Spain. Whatever his end, it is certain that Paul was a great influence on modern Christianity, both through his missionary work and his writing.

Apostle Paul's Contribution to Christianity

It has been said that if it were not for Paul and a few others such as Barnabas that Christianity would have remained a small unknown branch of Judaism. Paul was the leading missionary to the Gentiles (Non-Jewish). While many within the early church were determined that a Christian must first become a Jew, Paul insisted that this was not the case. He recognized that the message of Jesus was for all men. In a letter to the Galatians, he thoroughly spelled out a case for the message of Jesus being a "New Covenant" with humanity.

According to Paul, Abraham accepted God of his free will, and God favored Abraham for this reason. This was the covenant that God made with Abraham and his descendants. The laws given to Moses were not set down for another couple hundred years. So, Paul believed that they were not part of the original bargain, but were given later to Moses as an intermediate guide until Jesus came to set down the new "Law" and the New "Covenant".

Paul noted that Jesus died on the Cross not only for our sins but to take on the burden of Mosaic Law. Thus, a Christian need not first become a Jew in order to follow Jesus. This was revealed when he commented that like Abraham Christians are saved by their faith alone. The zeal Paul used to persecute Christians was changed. He did all that he could to discourage the issue of separating Jews from Gentiles by means of his vivid interpretation of the word of God to the various churches. Paul, himself, seems to have been of the opinion that faith was all that was required.

He succeeded in making Christianity a universal religion, not just in the spiritual sense but also in the physical sense. Spreading the Gospel far and wide across the Roman Empire was Paul's mission. His missionary journeys brought him to Asia Minor, Greece, Macedonia and eventually Rome.

There is no question that his Roman citizenship and his intense training as a Pharisee helped him immensely in this mission. He was arrested several times because of his preaching and several times was saved because of his elevated status within the Empire.

Besides being a fiery orator, Paul was also a capable writer. His letters make up the bulk of the epistles in the Bible. Because his writings were so treasured, they are among the most studied today. The words of Paul carry weight far greater than those of James or Peter, some of whose letters also survive. Paul's thoughtfulness, gentleness and steadfastness infuse his letters and they also infuse the close adherents of his words today.

Paul was a charismatic individual. He was a sure leader of men. Seldom did he doubt himself. He saw his mission as not only bringing the "Good News" to the Gentiles, but also to organize the Church so that it would grow, even when he was not present to urge it on. Thus, he created an organization and trained leaders. This organization would one day become modern Christianity as it came to supersede the original authority of the Church in Jerusalem.

Conclusion

Paul's life and mission were profoundly shaped by his dramatic encounter with Christ on the Road to Damascus. This transformative event, combined with Paul's unwavering zeal, became the driving force that shaped the trajectory of Christianity for centuries to come. Through the lens of Paul's teachings, Christians today continue to understand and experience Christ's message.

Paul played a crucial role in establishing Christianity as a "universal" church, both physically through his missionary journeys and theologically through his epistles. His letters, often referred to as the Epistles of the Apostle Paul, serve as an essential appendix to the teachings of the Gospel. These writings should be a focal point for anyone seeking a deeper understanding of the Christian faith. The epistles stand out for their profoundly elevated religious thought, showcasing Paul's deep scholarship in the Old Testament and his profound grasp of Christ's teachings as presented in the New Testament.

The Acts of the Apostles, one of the original sources of Christian history, offers a detailed account of Paul's life and ministry. Some scholars suggest that Acts may have been intended as a legal brief, drawn from Paul's recollections and Luke's diary, to support Paul's defense during his trial before the Emperor. However, it is noteworthy that neither the Acts of the Apostles nor Paul's surviving letters provide a detailed account of the outcome of his trial, leaving the final chapter of Paul's earthly life shrouded in mystery.

DR. MAXWELL SHIMBA

APOSTLE PAUL'S PARENTS

Who Was Apostle Paul and Who Were His Parents?

Despite being born in a city deeply influenced by Greek culture and firmly integrated into the Roman Empire, Saul—who would later become known as Paul—was raised in the nurturing embrace of a devout Hebrew family. This Hebrew identity was not merely a cultural label; it profoundly shaped the very core of his existence.

In the early stages of Paul's life, the overwhelming presence of Roman authority and Greek philosophy did not define his upbringing. Instead, he was raised as an Israelite child, deeply immersed in the sacred narratives of his people. These stories, central to Jewish faith and tradition, became the foundation of his teachings in the synagogues, where he would later revisit these ancient tales with newfound depth, enriched by the life, death, and resurrection of the crucified Messiah (as reflected in Acts 13:16-41, 17:2-3, 10-11, 28:23).

While history offers only glimpses of Paul's mother, leaving us with more questions than answers, we do know that Paul's father was a figure of some prominence in his life. However, Paul's mother remains largely a mystery. Paul does allude to his divine calling, describing himself as one set apart by God "from his mother's womb" (Galatians 1:15). This suggests that even from birth, Paul's life was destined for a higher purpose—one that would eventually lead him to proclaim the message of the crucified Messiah to the Gentiles. Yet, beyond this brief and cryptic reference, little is known about the woman who played a crucial role in the early life of the Apostle.

We do find mention of Paul's sister and her son (Acts 23:16), as well as other relatives (Romans 16:7, 11, 21). Yet, oddly, the one who likely held the closest familial bond with him—his mother—remains absent from the historical record. Paul openly acknowledges his teacher, the esteemed Rabbi Gamaliel, but he never speaks of the person who, if she had lived, would have been his first and most influential teacher.

The fate of Paul's mother is obscured by the veil of history. Did she, like Rachel—the mother of Benjamin and the revered matriarch of his tribe—die in childbirth, leaving Paul's father to mourn her loss and perhaps even commemorate her in some enduring way, much like Jacob's tribute near Bethlehem (Genesis 35:16-20, 48:7)? Or did she survive to witness her son's dramatic shift from Pharisaic zealot to Christian apostle, passing away before she could reconcile herself to his newfound faith? Perhaps, in a more hopeful scenario, she accepted and believed in the Savior whom her son would come to serve with such fervor.

The life and legacy of Paul's mother remain hidden in the annals of history, leaving us to speculate about her journey, her beliefs, and her influence on the man who would become one of Christianity's greatest apostles. Her story, though untold, undoubtedly played a crucial role in shaping the destiny of Paul, the Apostle to the Gentiles.

The questions surrounding Paul's family remain shrouded in the mists of time, their answers eluding us. To catch a glimpse of the apostle's earliest days, we must content ourselves with a simple image—a Jewish mother and her child. Such an image echoes in the brief narrative of Elizabeth and John the Baptist, and while one Gospel may lack certain details, the other offers some pieces to complete the picture.

The precise moment of Paul's birth within his family remains a mystery. Some have suggested, based on a sermon attributed to St. Chrysostom, that he was born in the year 2 B.C. in our reckoning. While this date is plausible, the authenticity of the sermon is questioned, and even if it were indeed the work of the eloquent Father, there's no assurance he possessed definitive information. Yet, we need not be overly concerned with this particular detail, for we have a richer chronology than mere years and months.

What we do know is that Paul was a young man when Stephen faced martyrdom. Consequently, we gain insight into the characteristics of the era and the world's circumstances at the outset of his remarkable life. He likely entered the world during the latter years of Herod's reign or the early years of his son Archelaus's rule. It marked the zenith of Augustus's powerful reign.

The world enjoyed an era of peace, and the Levant's pirates had been vanquished, while Cilicia, among other provinces, lay in repose or somnolence beneath the expansive shadow of Roman authority. Numerous governors had overseen the region since Cicero's time, and among them had been Athenodorus, the emperor's mentor.

This was the time when luminaries like Horace and Maecenas departed from the world, their names forever etched in history. Simultaneously, it witnessed the birth of Caligula and others destined to inflict misery upon the world. It is through such landmarks that we fix the epoch in a manner most relatable to the human imagination. It was during this pause in the tapestry of world history that Paul came into existence.

The same profound joy that accompanied Paul's birth within his family and the celebratory naming of a son in the "hill country" of Judea, as chronicled in Luke 1:39, also resonated among the Jews of the diaspora. Just as the "neighbors and cousins" of Elizabeth "heard how the Lord had showed great mercy upon her, and rejoiced with her," a similar spirit of elation filled the household in Tarsus when Saul was born.

In a nation where the promise of a Messiah's birth hung in the air, and at a time when the longing for the fulfillment of this promise grew increasingly fervent and palpable, the birth of a son was the realization of a mother's deepest bliss. To the father as well, one might paraphrase the words of Jeremiah, saying, "Blessed is the man who brings tidings, declaring, 'A man child is born unto you,'" filling his heart with gladness (Jeremiah 20:15).

On the eighth day following his birth, the infant Saul, soon to be known as Paul, underwent the sacred rite of circumcision and received his name. When the query regarding a name was put forth to his father as the head of the family, he gave his consent, in obedience to the divine vision. Naming a Jewish child after his father was not uncommon. However, it was also a prevailing tradition, throughout Jewish history, even in the absence of prophetic guidance, to select a name reflective of religious sentiment.

As the infant in Tarsus was bestowed with the name Saul, which would ultimately transform into Paul, it might have been chosen "after the name of his father." Furthermore, it was a name steeped in tradition and held in high esteem within the tribe of Benjamin, for it was the name of the first king anointed by the prophet Samuel. Alternatively, when his father proclaimed "his name is Saul," it could have symbolized (in accordance with the Hebrew derivation of the word) that he was a cherished son, longed for with great fervor, the firstborn of his family—a child of prayer consecrated to God, much like the prophet Samuel himself.

INTRODUCTION

SETTING THE STAGE FOR THE SIGNIFICANCE OF APOSTLE PAUL

In the chronicles of early Christianity, few figures stand as prominently as the enigmatic and influential Apostle Paul. Born Saul of Tarsus, Paul's journey from a zealous persecutor of Christians to one of the faith's most ardent advocates is a compelling story of transformation. In this introductory chapter, we embark on an exploration of Paul's life, uncovering the pivotal role he played in shaping the course of Christianity.

The first century AD was a time of great upheaval, with the Roman Empire dominating vast territories and religious landscapes in constant flux. Against this backdrop, Paul emerged as a critical link between Judaism and the burgeoning Christian movement. His teachings, letters, and relentless missionary work planted the seeds of a faith that would endure for millennia.

As we delve into the life of Apostle Paul, we will explore the rich tapestry of his early years in Tarsus, the life-altering encounter on the road to Damascus, and the profound theological contributions he made to Christian thought. We will journey with him through the ancient Mediterranean world, witnessing the trials and triumphs of his missionary endeavors and the controversies that shaped his legacy.

Furthermore, this journey will allow us to grasp the essence of Paul's teachings, from his emphasis on grace and faith to his ethical instructions for early Christian communities. We will examine his interactions with other key figures of his time, including the apostles in Jerusalem, and his pivotal role in addressing critical issues like the inclusion of Gentiles in the Christian fold.

Apostle Paul's life is far more than a mere historical account; it is a profound story of faith, transformation, and an unwavering dedication to his divine mission. His legacy is deeply embedded not only in the pages of the New Testament but also in the very foundations of Christian doctrine, shaping the core beliefs and practices that define Christianity today.

As we journey through the chapters that follow, we will delve into the many dimensions of this extraordinary figure, peeling back the layers of history to reveal the complexities of his character, the depth of his convictions, and the far-reaching impact of his work. We will explore Paul's relentless pursuit of his mission, from his early days as a fervent Pharisee to his dramatic conversion on the road to Damascus, and his tireless efforts to spread the Gospel across the Roman Empire.

This exploration will take us through Paul's missionary journeys, his theological contributions, and the personal sacrifices he made in the name of Christ. We will examine how his letters continue to inspire and guide Christians around the world, and how his teachings have shaped the course of

Christian thought for centuries. Join us on this journey through time and faith as we uncover the life and enduring legacy of Apostle Paul, a man whose impact on Christianity is as profound today as it was nearly two thousand years ago.

CHAPTER 1

APOSTLE PAUL IN THE EARLY CHRISTIAN MOVEMENT

Understanding the Significance of Apostle Paul in the Early Christian Movement

To grasp the profound significance of Apostle Paul in the early Christian movement, we must first immerse ourselves in the rich historical and religious tapestry of the first century AD. This era was a pivotal moment in human history, marked by a convergence of events and ideas that would shape the course of civilizations for millennia to come.

The Roman Empire

At the heart of this period stood the formidable Roman Empire, a vast and powerful entity that stretched from the British Isles to the banks of the Nile, and from Hispania to the far reaches of the Middle East. The Roman Empire was an unparalleled force in terms of military conquests, architectural and engineering marvels, and administrative sophistication. Its legions were renowned for their discipline and effectiveness, its roads and aqueducts for their ingenuity, and its governance for its ability to maintain order over such an expansive territory. Yet, despite its might, the empire was not without its challenges. Social and political upheaval simmered beneath the surface, as diverse cultures and peoples were brought under Roman rule, often leading to tensions and unrest.

Religious Diversity

Religion was a central aspect of life throughout the Roman Empire, deeply intertwined with daily existence and civic identity. The prevailing religious landscape was polytheistic, with a vast pantheon of gods and goddesses worshipped across the empire. Temples dedicated to these deities dotted the landscape, and religious rituals were integral to public and private life. In addition to the traditional Roman gods, the empire was a melting pot of religious practices, influenced by the diverse cultures within its borders. Cults and mystery religions, such as those dedicated to Mithras and Isis, promised personal salvation and spiritual fulfillment, attracting followers who sought deeper religious experiences beyond the state-sanctioned practices.

Judaism in the First Century

In the province of Judea, amid the grandeur of the Roman Empire, a unique monotheistic faith—Judaism—held a central place. The Jewish people, despite living under Roman occupation, maintained a strong religious identity rooted in their covenant with the one true God, Yahweh. Jerusalem, the spiritual and cultural heart of Judaism, was home to the magnificent Temple, where sacrifices and festivals were observed according to the Law of Moses.

The Jewish community of this time was marked by a deep sense of expectation and hope. Many Jews longed for the arrival of the Messiah, a deliverer prophesied in their sacred scriptures, who would restore Israel and liberate them from the yoke of Roman oppression. This messianic hope was a powerful undercurrent in Jewish society, influencing various movements and sects, including the Pharisees, Sadducees, Essenes, and Zealots. Each group had its own interpretation of how to live out the covenant with God under Roman rule and its own vision of what the coming of the Messiah would entail.

The Convergence of Cultures and Ideas

It was within this complex and dynamic environment that the early Christian movement began to take shape. The teachings of Jesus of Nazareth, a Jewish teacher and healer, had stirred the hearts of many, and His message of the Kingdom of God resonated with those who longed for spiritual renewal and social justice. After His crucifixion and resurrection, as recorded in the Gospels, His followers, known as Christians, began to spread His teachings throughout Judea and beyond. This was the world into which Saul of Tarsus, later known as Paul, was born—a world where the intersection of Roman power, Jewish tradition, and diverse religious thought created a fertile ground for the emergence of a new faith.

Apostle Paul's Role in the Christian Movement

Paul, originally a devout Pharisee and a zealous persecutor of Christians, would undergo a dramatic transformation following his encounter with the risen Christ on the road to Damascus (Acts 9:3-6). This event marked the beginning of his mission to spread the Gospel to the Gentiles, breaking down the barriers between Jews and non-Jews and helping to establish Christianity as a universal faith. Paul's deep understanding of Jewish law and scripture, combined with his Roman citizenship and knowledge of Greek culture, uniquely positioned him to bridge the gap between the Jewish roots of Christianity and the broader Greco-Roman world.

In his letters, Paul articulated key theological concepts that would become foundational to Christian doctrine, such as justification by faith, the role of grace, and the universality of Christ's salvation. His writings, which form a significant portion of the New Testament, continue to be a source of theological insight and spiritual guidance for Christians around the world.

As we explore the life and legacy of Apostle Paul, we will see how his efforts, inspired by his profound faith and commitment to Christ, were instrumental in shaping the early Christian movement. His work helped to transform Christianity from a small sect within Judaism into a global faith that transcended cultural and ethnic boundaries, fulfilling the promise that in Christ, "There is neither Jew nor Greek, there is neither slave nor free, there is neither male nor female; for you are all one in Christ Jesus" (Galatians 3:28). This exploration will take us deeper into the historical, cultural, and religious contexts that influenced Paul's mission, providing a richer understanding of his pivotal role in the history of Christianity.

Paul's Significance in the Early Christian Movement:

Amidst this complex religious and political landscape, a small but rapidly growing religious sect known as Christianity emerged. It centered its beliefs on the life and teachings of Jesus of Nazareth, whom many considered the prophesied Messiah. It was into this milieu that Saul of Tarsus, later known as Paul, was born and would play a transformative role.

Paul's significance in the early Christian movement was multifaceted. He was a Pharisee, deeply steeped in Jewish traditions, but his dramatic conversion on the road to Damascus would lead him to become one of Christianity's most passionate advocates. Paul's theological insights, articulated in his letters, would shape the foundations of Christian doctrine, emphasizing concepts like grace, faith, and justification.

As we journey through this book, we will unravel the life, teachings, and impact of Apostle Paul. We will witness how his unique position as a bridge between Judaism and Christianity, combined with his fervent missionary efforts, would leave an indelible mark on the faith, forever altering the course of Christianity's evolution. In the chapters that follow, we will delve deeper into the life and times of this remarkable figure, exploring the circumstances that led to his conversion and the subsequent legacy he left for generations to come.

Setting the Historical and Religious Context of the First Century AD

The Roman Empire

The first century AD was a time dominated by the Roman Empire, a colossal force that ruled over vast territories stretching from Britain in the west to Egypt in the east. The empire was not only a military and political powerhouse but also a cultural juggernaut that profoundly influenced the regions under its control. The impact of Roman rule is evident throughout the New Testament, as seen in the Gospel of Luke, where Caesar Augustus issues a decree for a census, compelling Mary and Joseph to travel to Bethlehem (Luke 2:1-5). This decree, issued from the heart of the Roman Empire, exemplifies the far-reaching authority of Rome and its influence on the daily lives of people throughout its provinces.

Religious Diversity within the Empire

The Roman Empire was a melting pot of religious beliefs and practices, with a diverse array of gods, cults, and spiritual traditions coexisting within its borders. This pluralistic environment is vividly depicted in the book of Acts, where the Apostle Paul encounters the religious diversity of Athens. There, he finds an altar dedicated to an "unknown god," symbolizing the Athenians' attempts to cover all spiritual bases in a world filled with countless deities (Acts 17:22-23). This encounter underscores the religious pluralism of the time, as well as the challenges and opportunities it presented for the early Christian missionaries who sought to proclaim the message of Christ in such a diverse context.

Judaism in Judea

In the province of Judea, Judaism stood out as a unique monotheistic faith amidst the polytheistic landscape of the Roman Empire. The Jewish people maintained a strong religious identity, centered around their belief in one God, Yahweh, and the sacred texts that recorded His covenant with Israel. This period was marked by a fervent expectation of the Messiah, a promised deliverer who would restore Israel and fulfill the ancient prophecies. These messianic hopes are woven throughout the New Testament, with references to prophetic passages such as Isaiah 9:6-7, which foretells the birth of a ruler who will establish a kingdom of justice and righteousness, and Micah 5:2, which predicts the birthplace of this ruler in Bethlehem.

The Pharisees, Sadducees, and Zealots

Within Judaism, various sects played significant roles in the religious landscape of the first century. The Pharisees and Sadducees were two of the most prominent groups, each with its own interpretation of the Torah and its role in Jewish life. The Pharisees, known for their strict adherence to the Law, often clashed with Jesus, questioning His teachings and authority, as seen in passages like Matthew 22:34-40. The

Sadducees, on the other hand, were more aligned with the temple priesthood and tended to be more conservative in their religious views, particularly in their denial of the resurrection, which became a point of contention with Jesus and His followers.

The Zealots were another significant group, characterized by their fierce opposition to Roman rule. They believed in the violent overthrow of the Roman occupiers as a means to achieve Jewish independence. One of Jesus' own disciples, Simon, was known as "Simon the Zealot," highlighting the diverse backgrounds of those who followed Jesus (Luke 6:15).

The Ministry of Jesus

Jesus of Nazareth began His public ministry in the early first century AD, preaching throughout Galilee and Judea. His teachings, often delivered in parables, resonated with the common people and challenged the religious authorities of His time. The Sermon on the Mount (Matthew 5-7) is one of the most famous discourses of Jesus, offering a radical reinterpretation of the Law that emphasized inner purity and moral integrity. The Parables of the Kingdom (Matthew 13) provide profound insights into the nature of God's Kingdom, illustrating spiritual truths through everyday stories.

The Early Christian Community

Following Jesus' resurrection and ascension, His followers formed the early Christian community, which quickly began to grow despite facing significant opposition. The New Testament documents the emergence of this community, particularly in the book of Acts. The day of Pentecost, as described in Acts 2, marks a critical moment in the birth of the Christian Church, when the Holy Spirit was poured out on the apostles, empowering them to preach the Gospel with boldness. This event led to the conversion of thousands and the rapid expansion of the Christian faith.

Persecution of Christians

As the early Christian movement gained momentum, it also faced intense persecution from both Jewish and Roman authorities. The New Testament recounts the story of Saul of Tarsus, who was initially a fervent persecutor of Christians. He was present at the stoning of Stephen, the first Christian martyr, and continued to hunt down believers with zeal (Acts 8:1-3). However, on the road to Damascus, Saul experienced a dramatic conversion, encountering the risen Christ and becoming the Apostle Paul, one of the most influential figures in the spread of Christianity (Acts 9:1-19).

The Spread of Christianity

The spread of Christianity beyond Judea is a central theme in the book of Acts, particularly through the missionary journeys of Paul. His travels took him across the Roman Empire, from Asia Minor to Greece and eventually to Rome itself. Acts 13-28 chronicles these journeys, detailing Paul's efforts to establish Christian communities, engage with diverse audiences, and address the theological and practical challenges facing the early Church. Paul's letters, written to the churches he founded, are some of the most important documents in the New Testament, offering insights into the early Christian faith and its development.

The Significance of Apostle Paul

Understanding the historical and religious context of the first century AD is crucial for appreciating the significance of Apostle Paul in the early Christian movement. His contributions to the spread of Christianity, his theological insights, and his missionary zeal were instrumental in shaping the course of Christian history. Paul's dramatic conversion on the road to Damascus, followed by his tireless efforts to preach the Gospel to both Jews and Gentiles, marks him as a pivotal figure in the establishment of Christianity as a global faith. His letters continue to be studied and revered for their profound theological content, reflecting a deep understanding of both Jewish tradition and the teachings of Christ. Through his life and work, Paul helped to lay the foundations of a faith that would endure and thrive for centuries to come.

Theological Contributions of Apostle Paul

Apostle Paul's letters, known as epistles, form a cornerstone of the New Testament and provide some of the most profound theological insights into Christianity. His writings delve deeply into the nature of salvation, the role of faith, and the moral and spiritual life of believers.

In his letter to the Romans, Paul offers an extensive exposition on the concept of justification by faith. He argues that righteousness comes through faith in Jesus Christ, apart from the works of the Law (Romans 3:21-26). This teaching laid the foundation for the doctrine of salvation by grace, emphasizing that God's grace, not human effort, is the basis of salvation (Romans 5:8). This idea of grace as a free and unearned gift is a central tenet of Christian theology and has had a lasting impact on the understanding of the relationship between God and humanity.

In 1 Corinthians, Paul addresses the essential Christian virtue of love, famously describing it as the greatest of all gifts (1 Corinthians 13). His poetic and powerful description of love as patient, kind, and enduring has become one of the most beloved passages in the Bible and is often cited in discussions of Christian ethics and interpersonal relationships. Additionally, Paul's discourse on the resurrection of the dead in 1 Corinthians 15 provides a comprehensive theological framework for understanding the resurrection of Christ and the future resurrection of believers, affirming the hope of eternal life that lies at the heart of the Christian faith.

Inclusion of Gentiles in the Christian Community

One of Paul's most significant contributions to the early Christian movement was his advocacy for the inclusion of Gentiles (non-Jews) in the Christian community without requiring them to adhere to Jewish customs such as circumcision. This was a revolutionary stance in a time when Christianity was still closely linked to Judaism and its traditions.

The issue of Gentile inclusion came to a head during the Jerusalem Council, as recorded in Acts 15. Here, Paul argued that faith in Christ was sufficient for salvation and that Gentile converts should not be burdened with the requirements of the Mosaic Law (Acts 15:6-21). His position was ultimately supported by the council, marking a decisive moment in the history of Christianity that opened the door for its expansion into the broader Greco-Roman world. This decision helped to establish Christianity as a universal faith, accessible to all people regardless of their cultural or ethnic background.

Conflict Resolution and Leadership in the Early Church

Paul's epistles, particularly 1 and 2 Corinthians, Galatians, and Philippians, frequently address the challenges and conflicts that arose within the early Christian communities. His letters offer guidance on a wide range of issues, from disputes over ethical behavior to questions of church unity and leadership.

In 1 Corinthians, for example, Paul addresses divisions within the church at Corinth, urging believers to be united in mind and purpose (1 Corinthians 1:10). He also provides practical advice on issues such as marriage, spiritual gifts, and the proper conduct of communal worship. In Galatians, Paul confronts the issue of legalism, warning against those who would impose the Jewish Law on Gentile converts, and passionately defends the doctrine of justification by faith alone (Galatians 2:15-21).

Paul's leadership was characterized by his pastoral concern for the communities he founded and his willingness to confront difficult issues head-on. His letters often reflect his deep love for the believers, his commitment to their spiritual growth, and his desire to see them live out the gospel in their daily lives.

Martyrdom and Endurance

Paul's mission to spread the Gospel was marked by significant hardships, including imprisonments, beatings, and shipwrecks. In his second letter to the Corinthians, he recounts the many trials he endured for the sake of Christ, including receiving 39 lashes on five separate occasions, being beaten with rods, stoned, shipwrecked, and facing dangers from both Jews and Gentiles (2 Corinthians 11:24-27).

Despite these adversities, Paul remained steadfast in his faith and undeterred in his mission. Even while imprisoned, he continued to write letters to the churches, offering encouragement, instruction, and theological insights. The letters to the Ephesians, Philippians, Colossians, and Philemon, often referred to as the "Prison Epistles," were written during his imprisonment and demonstrate his unwavering commitment to his calling and his deep concern for the wellbeing of the Christian communities.

Legacy and Influence

The legacy of Apostle Paul is immeasurable. His writings continue to shape Christian theology, practice, and spiritual life. Paul's teachings on faith, grace, love, and Christian living are foundational to the Christian tradition, and his epistles remain a primary source of doctrinal and ethical guidance for believers around the world.

Moreover, Paul's example of unwavering faith, despite persecution and suffering, has inspired countless Christians throughout history. His missionary zeal and theological insights were instrumental in transforming Christianity from a small Jewish sect into a global faith that transcends cultural and ethnic boundaries.

Paul's role in the early Christian movement was transformative. His theological contributions, missionary efforts, and passionate advocacy for the inclusion of Gentiles were key factors in the spread of Christianity beyond its Jewish origins. His letters serve as enduring sources of wisdom and inspiration, and his legacy continues to be a cornerstone of Christian thought and practice, influencing the faith of millions across the centuries.

CHAPTER 02

EARLY LIFE IN TARSUS

Paul's Upbringing in Tarsus: A Multicultural City

The city of Tarsus, located in the southeastern region of Asia Minor (modern-day Turkey), was the backdrop for the early years of Saul of Tarsus, who would later become the Apostle Paul. Tarsus was no ordinary city; it was a vibrant and culturally diverse hub that played a crucial role in shaping the young Saul's worldview and intellectual development.

Tarsus: A Melting Pot of Cultures

In the first century AD, Tarsus was a thriving center of trade, commerce, and education. Its strategic position along the Mediterranean coast, coupled with its status as a free city under Roman rule, made it a melting pot of cultures and ideas. People from various ethnic and cultural backgrounds—including Greeks, Romans, Jews, and others—converged in Tarsus, bringing with them their languages, philosophies, and religious traditions. This cultural diversity exposed Saul to a wide range of ideas and perspectives from a young age, fostering in him a broad understanding of the world beyond his Jewish heritage.

Tarsus was also renowned for its intellectual climate. It was home to a famous university that rivaled those of Athens and Alexandria, attracting scholars and students from across the Roman Empire. The city's reputation as a center of learning meant that Saul grew up in an environment where philosophical debates and discussions were a part of daily life. This exposure to various schools of thought, including Stoicism and other Greco-Roman philosophies, would later influence his ability to engage with diverse audiences as he spread the Christian message.

Education as a Pharisee: A Rigorous Training

Despite the cosmopolitan nature of Tarsus, Saul's upbringing was deeply rooted in his Jewish identity, particularly in the traditions of the Pharisees, a prominent Jewish religious group known for their strict adherence to the Law of Moses and their dedication to the study of Scripture. Saul's family was likely devout and committed to Pharisaic teachings, ensuring that he received a thorough education in Jewish law, theology, and customs from an early age.

Saul's education would have been rigorous, involving intensive study of the Torah, the Prophets, and other sacred texts. He was trained to memorize large portions of Scripture, understand the nuances of Jewish law, and debate religious issues with precision and skill. This training was not just academic; it was also deeply spiritual, instilling in Saul a profound reverence for the traditions and commandments of his faith.

This Pharisaic education took place not only in Tarsus but also in Jerusalem, where Saul studied under the famous Rabbi Gamaliel, one of the most respected teachers of the time (Acts 22:3). Gamaliel's influence on Saul would have been significant, providing him with a deep and nuanced understanding of Jewish theology and an ability to interpret Scripture with great insight. This background equipped Saul with the intellectual tools and religious fervor that would later be pivotal in his role as a leader in the early Christian Church.

The Influence of Tarsus on Paul's Ministry

The multicultural and intellectual environment of Tarsus, combined with his Pharisaic upbringing, gave Paul a unique set of skills and perspectives that would be crucial in his later ministry. His ability to speak Greek fluently and his familiarity with Hellenistic culture allowed him to communicate effectively with Gentile audiences across the Roman Empire. Moreover, his deep knowledge of Jewish law and Scripture enabled him to engage with Jewish audiences and explain how the life and teachings of Jesus Christ fulfilled the prophecies of the Hebrew Bible.

Paul's dual identity as a Roman citizen and a devout Jew from a cosmopolitan city like Tarsus also gave him the flexibility to navigate the complex cultural and political landscapes of the Roman Empire. He could appeal to his Roman citizenship when necessary, as he did when he was arrested in Jerusalem (Acts 22:25-29), while also drawing on his Jewish heritage to establish his credibility as a teacher of the faith.

Paul's upbringing in Tarsus provided him with a rich tapestry of cultural, intellectual, and religious experiences that shaped him into one of the most influential figures in early Christianity. His ability to bridge different worlds—Jewish and Gentile, religious and philosophical—was key to his success in spreading the Gospel and establishing Christian communities throughout the Roman Empire.

Was Apostle Paul a Pharisee? What, then, constituted a Pharisee? A Pharisee was a man in whom the essence of religiosity ran deep—a staunch believer in divine revelation. He staunchly advocated for the authority of law, and consequently, government. By theoretical principles, he eschewed unbridled outbursts of passion. Professing a commitment to strict morality, he lived by its precepts. A zealous disseminator of religious doctrine, he clung tenaciously to his own beliefs, to the traditions of his forefathers, and to all aspects of religion, encompassing its rituals, ceremonies, and doctrines. Such a man was intolerant of opposing views but, if adhering to his principles, would have been a persecutor only within the bounds of the law and not driven by popular fervor. This was the paternal influence under which Saul of Tarsus was nurtured—a young man who, instead of actively participating in persecution, found himself "keeping the raiment" of those who, in disregard of all legal norms, were fervently engaged in a deadly mission.

Additionally, there was another aspect of his father's life that may shed light on Paul's subsequent journey. It pertained to his father's relationship with the Roman government. Though a Jew of pure lineage, so much so that Paul could later declare himself "an Hebrew of the Hebrews" (Philippians 3:6), his father, as was not uncommon for foreigners, had secured the privileges of Roman citizenship. Thus, when seeking refuge from persecution at the hands of his fellow countrymen by appealing to Roman authorities, he could assert, "I was freeborn," indicating that he possessed the inherent right to protection under Roman law (Acts 22:28).

The manner in which his father acquired this citizenship, whether through purchase, as in the case of the "chief captain" to whom Paul appealed, or as a reward for some service rendered to the Roman cause during civil conflicts (which seems more likely), remains shrouded in obscurity and is beyond our reach to determine. However, whatever the means, it was undoubtedly regarded as a prestigious distinction among Jews—a source of safety in times of peril and a guarantee, akin to a modern-day passport, of security throughout the expanse of the Roman Empire. Paul, on multiple occasions, invoked this status as a shield against danger, and by virtue of it, he eventually escalated his case from Hebrew tribunals, even proconsular ones, to the very Emperor himself (Acts 16:37; 22:25-29; 25:10-11).

Regarding his place of birth, another noteworthy detail concerning Saul's upbringing, one that bears significance in light of his divine calling, is that he received his early education in a city with strong Greek influences. Tarsus, located in Cilicia along the banks of the Cydnus River, maintained a thriving commerce and was renowned for its Greek philosophy and literature. In fact, it was so academically distinguished that Strabo, the geographer, ranked it alongside Athens and Alexandria in terms of scholarly prominence (Strabo, XIV, pp. 673, 674).

While today it stands as a modest town inhabited by Turks, numbering no more than thirty thousand residents, during Paul's youth, Tarsus was a bustling hub of trade. St. Basil records that "Tarsus was a point of union for Syrians, Cilicians, Isaurians, and Cappadocians." It drew Greek and Roman merchants and hosted a diverse array of people, each clad in the distinct attire of their respective regions. Young Saul, amidst the bustling wharves of the Cydnus, would have interacted with individuals from nearly every corner of the known world.

Indeed, he was a Jewish boy, and undoubtedly received instruction and education in Jewish schools under Jewish influence. However, there exists another form of education beyond what one garners from textbooks and lessons. It's the education of one's surroundings, peers, playmates, the language spoken in their milieu, and the literature they encounter. These elements are inextricably linked, each influencing the character of an educated youth in ways that are challenging to dissect. What one absorbs from external influences can often prove as consequential, if not more so, than the lessons instilled at home and in the classroom.

Under the guidance of his father, a devout Hebrew, Saul would have been schooled in Hebrew letters and learning. Following the wisdom of Jewish tradition, he was also taught a "trade"—in his case, that of a "tent-maker" (Acts 18:3). However, he dwelt among a Greek populace, conversed with those who spoke the Greek tongue, and, directly or indirectly, became acquainted with Greek literature to varying degrees. His later adept and fitting references to Greek poets (Acts 17:28; Titus 1:12; 1 Corinthians 15:33) demonstrate that he was not a stranger to Greek learning in his formative years.

The implications of this upbringing on his future as an apostle are readily discernible. Greek was the lingua franca across the regions where he would travel. Most of his public discourses would be delivered in that language. All his written works, intended for preservation in the Church and the broader world, would be composed in Greek. He would encounter Greeks everywhere, preaching to them, elucidating the new faith, and defending it before them. He would stand among their philosophers, "engaging" their thinkers on their own intellectual turf.

Another pivotal aspect of Saul's early life was his tutelage under Gamaliel. Saul himself attests to this in Acts 22:3, stating that he was "brought up" or nurtured in Jerusalem "at the feet of Gamaliel" and was instructed in the meticulous observance of the ancestral law. This phraseology suggests that he had been placed under Gamaliel's guidance from a relatively young age. This implication is further reinforced by another expression he employs in Acts 26:4, describing his "manner of life from my youth" and stating that it was "at the first" among his own people in Jerusalem. According to Jewish custom, children were required to be taught the "law" by the age of thirteen.

The reason for Saul's presence in Jerusalem is clear. It was a decision made by his Jewish father, a Pharisee, who intended for his son to receive the most comprehensive instruction in the law. To accomplish this, he entrusted Saul to the tutelage of the most renowned Jewish teacher of that era. Gamaliel held a position of prominence among the Jews, similar to the status of Thomas Aquinas, Duns Scotus, and Bonaventure among the Schoolmen. Gamaliel was even bestowed with the title "the Beauty of the Law." Additionally, it is plausible that Saul's father may have wished to remove him, during his formative years, from influences in a Greek city that could potentially weaken his attachment to the Hebrew faith.

Gamaliel's character bore distinct features that left an indelible mark on Saul:

(a) Gamaliel was known for his fairness and judiciousness. A remarkable illustration of this trait can be found in his defense of the Apostles as documented in Acts 5:34-40. Despite the Sanhedrin's determination to condemn the apostles to death, it required significant courage to even stand up and argue their case, as it would expose one to accusations of supporting them. Gamaliel, however, with his character, competence, and position, commanded respect, and his counsel was eminently prudent, wise, and sensible. He quelled the Sanhedrin's fury and secured the release of the persecuted men. Although a Pharisee, he was not confined by the narrow biases of his faction. He dared to act according to principles of justice and truth. Such a man had earned the trust of his compatriots, and it is not surprising that he was "held in high esteem by all the people" (Acts 5:34). He belonged to the same class as Joseph of Arimathea and Nicodemus—a deeply religious man, a devoted Jew, a fervent Pharisee in contrast to other Jewish sects. Yet, he was a man of noble principles and a proficient mentor capable of instilling broad and liberal perspectives.

(b) Tradition has depicted him as a man who surpassed most of his fellow countrymen in his proficiency in Greek learning and his respect for it. If this is accurate, then his own mentality would have been broadened by these studies. The influence of this on someone who had spent his early years in a Greek city and had some exposure to Greek authors can be readily imagined. It is evident how this might have affected a person who would later spend a significant portion of his public life in the very heart of Greek philosophy, learning, and influence.

(c) As a prominent Pharisee, he held a high regard for authority. He was an instructor of the law and an expounder of the law. He was a Jew through and through. Yet, in contrast to all forms of passion, tumults arising from such emotions, and unjust or tyrannical actions driven by mere whims or popular sentiment, he was a man who staunchly adhered to the principles of law and order.

(d) As far as we know, he did not convert to Christianity. Despite his openness, erudition, and the liberal influence that may have stemmed from Greek literature, it cannot be asserted that Gamaliel would never justify persecution. A prayer, thought to have been written by him or at least endorsed by him, suggests that he supported the punishment of apostates. However, if he were ever involved in persecution, we know that it would have been executed within the bounds of the law and under the aegis of public authority.

The influence of these character traits on Saul's entire public life is readily discernible, whether during his days as a Jewish persecutor or as a defender of the faith he initially sought to obliterate. One can perceive how he might sympathize with persecutors and garner trust in that regard. He refrained from overt acts of violence and lawlessness, yet under the imprimatur of the law, he could become, as he indeed was, one of the most ardent and feared adversaries of the Church.

There is always a potential moral hazard for a young person when, for the sake of education, wealth, or honor, they depart from the familiar confines and influences of the family circle. Saul of Tarsus was exposed to such perils when he left the comfort of his childhood home. He departed from his father's presence and immediate authority, venturing even to Jerusalem. Many young men, despite their religious upbringing, falter in such transitions, but many others, though the number of those who fail is substantial, remain steadfast. Their early virtues, their religious convictions, their reverence for the law and for religion, prevail and triumph in the new crucible of experience. Saul of Tarsus belonged to the latter category. In his old age, when he contemplated the possibility of imminent death, he looked back on this period and could declare of his moral character throughout his youth, "concerning the righteousness which is in the law, found blameless" (Philippians 3:6).

Thus, the influence of his early training was clear. This was the young Saul, as he emerges in the persecution of

Stephen—a devout Jew, a fervent Pharisee, a conscientious and religious young man of high moral character. He was restrained, then as he would be throughout his life, from committing acts of lawless violence, yet he was always ready to engage fervently in persecution whenever it.

In the next chapters, we will delve further into Saul's early life, examining the factors that contributed to his zeal for Judaism and his initial opposition to the burgeoning Christian movement. We will explore how this upbringing in Tarsus and his Pharisaic education set the stage for the remarkable transformation that would lead Saul to become the influential figure known as the Apostle Paul.

CHAPTER 03

SAUL'S CONVERSION ON THE ROAD TO DAMASCUS

The Dramatic Encounter with Jesus

The story of Saul's conversion on the road to Damascus is one of the most pivotal and dramatic moments in the history of early Christianity. This encounter with the risen Christ not only transformed Saul's life but also reshaped the trajectory of the entire Christian movement, turning a fervent persecutor of Christians into one of their greatest advocates.

The Journey to Damascus

As recounted in Acts 9:1-2, Saul of Tarsus was zealously persecuting the early Christian community. His reputation as a fierce opponent of the followers of "the Way," as Christianity was initially called, preceded him. Armed with the authority from the high priests, Saul was on his way to Damascus to arrest any Christians he could find and bring them back to Jerusalem for punishment. He was a devout Pharisee, committed to maintaining the purity of Judaism as he understood it, and he viewed the burgeoning Christian movement as a dangerous heresy that needed to be stamped out.

The Blinding Light

As Saul and his companions approached Damascus, an extraordinary event occurred. A blinding light from heaven suddenly enveloped Saul, stopping him in his tracks (Acts 9:3). This light was not just a physical phenomenon but a divine manifestation that overwhelmed Saul's senses, leaving him disoriented and blinded. The intensity of the experience was such that it knocked Saul to the ground, rendering him helpless. This moment of divine intervention was a direct confrontation with the reality of the risen Christ.

The Voice from Heaven

In the midst of the blinding light, Saul heard a voice calling his name twice: "Saul, Saul, why do you persecute me?" (Acts 9:4). The repetition of his name underscored the urgency and personal nature of the message. Confused and frightened, Saul asked, "Who are you, Lord?" The voice responded, "I am Jesus, whom you are persecuting" (Acts 9:5). This revelation was both shocking and transformative. In an instant, Saul realized that in persecuting the followers of Jesus, he was actually persecuting Jesus Himself. This was a profound moment of reckoning, as Saul was confronted with the truth that the one he had been opposing was indeed the Messiah, risen and glorified.

The Transformation from Saul to Paul

Saul's encounter with the risen Jesus was a turning point of unimaginable significance. This was not just a moment of conversion; it was a complete transformation of his identity, mission, and worldview. The man who had been a zealous defender of Jewish tradition now found himself called to be a proclaimer of the very faith he had sought to destroy.

Blindness and the Role of Ananias

Blinded by the light, Saul was led by his companions into Damascus, where he remained in darkness for three days, neither eating nor drinking, as he grappled with the implications of his encounter (Acts 9:8-9). During this time, the Lord appeared in a vision to a disciple named Ananias, instructing him to go to Saul. Ananias was understandably hesitant, knowing Saul's fearsome reputation, but he obeyed the Lord's command. When Ananias found Saul, he laid his hands on him and said, "Brother Saul, the Lord—Jesus, who appeared to you on the road as you were coming here—has sent me so that you may see again and be filled with the Holy Spirit" (Acts 9:17). Immediately, something like scales fell from Saul's eyes, and his sight was restored (Acts 9:18). This physical healing was symbolic of the spiritual enlightenment that had taken place within Saul. No longer blinded by his former zealotry, Saul now saw the truth of Jesus Christ.

Conversion and Baptism

Humbled and transformed by his experience, Saul was baptized and began his new life as a follower of Christ. Without delay, he started preaching in the synagogues of Damascus, proclaiming that Jesus is the Son of God (Acts 9:20). The very man who had come to Damascus to arrest Christians was now boldly declaring the divinity of Christ, much to the amazement of those who knew him. This sudden and radical transformation baffled many and marked the beginning of Saul's journey as Paul, the Apostle to the Gentiles.

The Impact of Saul's Conversion

The conversion of Saul to Paul was more than just a personal turning point; it was a divine intervention that had far-reaching implications for the spread of Christianity. Paul's unique background as a Roman citizen, a Jew, and a Pharisee equipped him to bridge the gap between Jewish and Gentile communities, making him a vital figure in the expansion of the Christian faith beyond its Jewish roots. His missionary journeys, theological insights, and epistles would become foundational to the early Church and remain central to Christian theology to this day.

As we explore the subsequent chapters of Paul's life, we will delve into the depth of his teachings, his relentless missionary work, and the enduring legacy he left behind. Paul's dramatic encounter with Jesus on the road to Damascus not only transformed his life but also changed the course of history, making him one of the most influential figures in the Christian tradition.

CHAPTER 04

THEOLOGICAL FOUNDATIONS

Paul's Theological Framework and Beliefs

The Apostle Paul's theological contributions are integral to the development of Christian thought and doctrine. His epistles offer profound insights into the nature of God, humanity, salvation, and the Christian life. Paul's theology is both rich and complex, weaving together the threads of his Jewish heritage with the revelation of Jesus Christ to create a cohesive and transformative vision of the Christian faith.

Monotheism and God's Sovereignty

Paul, rooted in the Jewish tradition, upheld the core belief in monotheism—the belief in one, all-powerful God. This conviction is central to his theology, where he emphasizes the sovereignty and supremacy of God over all creation. In Romans 11:36, Paul writes, "For from him and through him and to him are all things. To him be the glory forever. Amen." This verse encapsulates Paul's understanding of God as the ultimate source, sustainer, and purpose of everything in existence. God's sovereignty means that He is in control of all things, orchestrating the events of history and the lives of individuals according to His divine will. This belief underscores Paul's entire theological framework, where God is seen as both transcendent and immanent, involved in the workings of the world and in the lives of believers.

Sin and Humanity's Fallen Nature

A key aspect of Paul's theology is his understanding of human sinfulness and the fallen state of humanity. In Romans 3:23, he declares, "For all have sinned and fall short of the glory of God." This verse is foundational to Paul's teaching on the universal need for salvation. He believed that sin was not merely a series of bad actions but a fundamental aspect of human nature that separates people from God. Paul viewed sin as a pervasive and inescapable condition that affects all aspects of human life, rendering humanity incapable of achieving righteousness on its own. This understanding is crucial for Paul's presentation of the Gospel because it sets the stage for the necessity of divine intervention through Jesus Christ.

Paul's view of sin is deeply rooted in the Hebrew Scriptures, particularly the account of the Fall in Genesis 3, where Adam and Eve's disobedience leads to the corruption of human nature. In his letter to the Romans, Paul contrasts the disobedience of Adam with the obedience of Christ, highlighting how Christ's sacrificial death reverses the effects of the Fall and offers the possibility of redemption (Romans 5:12-19).

Salvation through Faith

One of Paul's most significant theological contributions is his teaching on salvation by grace through faith. In Ephesians 2:8-9, he articulates this central principle: "For by grace you have been saved through faith. And this is not your own doing; it is the gift of God, not a result of works, so that no one may boast." For Paul, salvation is a divine gift, not something that can be earned through human effort or adherence to the Law. This concept was revolutionary in its implications, especially for a Jewish audience that was accustomed to viewing righteousness in terms of obedience to the Mosaic Law.

Paul's emphasis on grace highlights the unmerited favor of God—His willingness to offer salvation to all, regardless of their past sins or social status. Faith, in Paul's theology, is the means by which individuals receive this grace. It is not merely intellectual assent but a deep, trust-filled response to God's offer of salvation through Jesus Christ. Paul's doctrine of salvation by grace through faith would later become a cornerstone of Protestant theology, particularly in the teachings of Martin Luther and the Reformation.

Justification by Faith

Closely related to Paul's teaching on salvation is his doctrine of justification by faith. In Romans 3:24-25, Paul explains that believers are "justified by his grace as a gift, through the redemption that is in Christ Jesus." Justification, in Paul's theology, refers to being declared righteous before God. This righteousness is not based on human merit but is imputed to believers through their faith in Christ. Paul contrasts this with the idea of earning righteousness through the Law, arguing that the Law, while good, is powerless to save because of human sinfulness (Romans 8:3-4).

Paul's understanding of justification is deeply tied to his Christology. In his letter to the Galatians, he insists that righteousness cannot be achieved through the Law but only through faith in Jesus Christ (Galatians 2:16). This teaching was particularly important for the early Christian communities, which were grappling with the relationship between the Jewish Law and the new covenant established by Christ. Paul's doctrine of justification by faith provided a theological basis for the inclusion of Gentiles in the Christian community, without requiring them to adhere to the Jewish Law.

The Role of Jesus Christ

Central to Paul's theology is the role of Jesus Christ as the Savior and Redeemer of humanity. In 1 Corinthians 15:3-4, Paul succinctly summarizes the Gospel: "Christ died for our sins in accordance with the Scriptures, that he was buried, that he was raised on the third day in accordance with the Scriptures." This passage reflects Paul's deep conviction that Jesus' death and resurrection are the pivotal events in God's plan for the redemption of the world.

For Paul, Jesus is both the fulfillment of the messianic prophecies of the Hebrew Scriptures and the inaugurator of a new covenant between God and humanity. He emphasizes the atoning work of Christ on the cross, which he views as the means by which humanity is reconciled to God. This reconciliation is not just a legal transaction but a restoration of the relationship between God and people, made possible through the sacrificial love of Christ. Paul's Christology also includes the belief in Jesus' divinity and His pre-existence, as seen in passages like Philippians 2:5-11, where Paul speaks of Christ's humility in taking on human form and His subsequent exaltation by God.

Life in the Spirit

Paul introduced the concept of "life in the Spirit" as a key element of Christian living. In Romans 8:9, he writes, "You, however, are not in the flesh but in the Spirit, if in fact the Spirit of God dwells in you." Paul contrasts life "in the flesh" with life "in the Spirit," using these terms to describe two different modes of existence. Life in the flesh refers to living according to sinful human nature, characterized by selfishness and disobedience to God. In contrast, life in the Spirit is marked by the presence of the Holy Spirit, who empowers believers to live righteous and godly lives.

The indwelling of the Holy Spirit is a transformative experience that changes the believer's identity and behavior. Paul teaches that the Spirit not only enables believers to overcome sin but also produces in them the "fruit of the Spirit"—qualities such as love, joy, peace, patience, kindness, goodness, faithfulness, gentleness, and self-control (Galatians 5:22-23). The Spirit also serves as a guarantee of the believer's future inheritance in Christ, providing assurance of salvation and eternal life.

The Resurrection of Believers

One of the most profound aspects of Paul's theology is his teaching on the resurrection of believers. In 1 Corinthians 15, Paul presents a detailed argument for the resurrection, asserting that it is central to the Christian faith. He argues that just as Christ was raised from the dead, so too will all believers be resurrected to eternal life. This resurrection is not merely a spiritual continuation of existence but involves the transformation of the physical body into a glorified state, fit for eternal life in God's presence.

Paul's teaching on the resurrection was intended to provide hope and encouragement to the early Christian communities, who were often facing persecution and death. By affirming the resurrection, Paul emphasized the victory of Christ over sin and death, offering believers the assurance that their faith and labor were not in vain (1 Corinthians 15:54-58).

Paul's theological framework laid the groundwork for many of the key doctrines of Christianity, including salvation by grace through faith, justification, sanctification, and the role of the Holy Spirit. His writings, infused with both Jewish tradition and the revelation of Christ, provided a comprehensive theological foundation that has continued to shape Christian thought and practice for nearly two millennia. Paul's letters to the early Christian communities are not only rich in theological content but also deeply pastoral, offering guidance, encouragement, and correction to believers seeking to live out their faith in a complex and often hostile world. Through his profound insights and unwavering commitment to the Gospel, Paul remains one of the most influential figures in the history of Christianity.

CHAPTER 05

PAUL'S FIRST MISSIONARY JOURNEY

The Beginning of Paul's Missionary Work in Cyprus and Asia Minor

Paul's first missionary journey, as detailed in the Book of Acts, represents a significant milestone in the early Christian movement. This journey marked the beginning of Paul's efforts to spread the Gospel far beyond the confines of Jerusalem and Judea, reaching into the wider Roman world. It was during this journey that Paul began to establish his reputation as a formidable apostle, theologian, and missionary, laying the foundation for the expansion of Christianity across the Mediterranean.

The Journey Begins (Acts 13:1-3)

The first missionary journey began in the city of Antioch, a major center of early Christianity. Antioch, located in modern-day Turkey, was one of the most important cities in the Roman Empire and served as a launching point for missionary efforts. According to Acts 13:1-3, the church in Antioch was a vibrant community of believers that included prophets and teachers such as Barnabas, Simeon called Niger, Lucius of Cyrene, Manaen (who had been brought up with Herod the Tetrarch), and Saul (later known as Paul).

While the believers were worshiping the Lord and fasting, the Holy Spirit spoke to them, instructing them to "set apart for me Barnabas and Saul for the work to which I have called them" (Acts 13:2). This divine commissioning marked the official beginning of Paul's missionary work. After further fasting and prayer, the church laid hands on Paul and Barnabas and sent them off with their blessing. This act of commissioning was significant, as it demonstrated the unity and support of the Antioch church for Paul and Barnabas as they embarked on their mission.

Cyprus – Barnabas's Homeland (Acts 13:4-12)

The first destination on their journey was the island of Cyprus, which was familiar territory for Barnabas, as it was his homeland (Acts 4:36). Cyprus was a strategic choice, as it was located along major trade routes and had a sizable Jewish population. Upon arriving in Salamis, a major city on the island's eastern coast, Paul and Barnabas began preaching the Word of God in the synagogues, following their usual practice of starting with the Jewish community (Acts 13:5).

Their mission in Cyprus took a significant turn in Paphos, the capital of the island, where they encountered a Jewish sorcerer and false prophet named Bar-Jesus, also known as Elymas. Elymas was an attendant of Sergius Paulus, the Roman proconsul, who was described as an intelligent man interested in hearing the Word of God (Acts 13:7). However, Elymas attempted to turn the proconsul away from the faith. In a dramatic confrontation, Paul, filled with the Holy Spirit, rebuked Elymas, declaring, "You are a child of the devil and an enemy of everything that is right!" (Acts 13:10). Paul then pronounced a temporary blindness on Elymas, a judgment that immediately came to pass. Witnessing this miracle, Sergius Paulus was astonished and believed in the Lord (Acts 13:12). This event not only demonstrated the power of the Gospel over deceit and opposition but also marked a significant early success in Paul's missionary efforts.

Pisidian Antioch – Facing Opposition (Acts 13:13-52)

After leaving Cyprus, Paul, Barnabas, and their companion John Mark sailed to Perga in Pamphylia, where

John Mark departed from them and returned to Jerusalem (Acts 13:13). Paul and Barnabas continued their journey to Pisidian Antioch, a major city in Asia Minor (modern-day Turkey). Pisidian Antioch was a Roman colony and an important center of administration and commerce. As was their custom, Paul and Barnabas attended the synagogue on the Sabbath. After the reading of the Law and the Prophets, the synagogue rulers invited them to speak, offering Paul an opportunity to address the congregation (Acts 13:14-15).

Paul delivered a powerful sermon, tracing the history of Israel from the Exodus to the reign of King David, and declaring that Jesus was the promised Savior, the fulfillment of God's covenant with Israel (Acts 13:16-41). He emphasized the resurrection of Jesus as the decisive proof of His divine identity and the cornerstone of Christian faith. Paul's message was well-received by many in the congregation, and he and Barnabas were invited to speak again on the following Sabbath.

However, the positive response soon provoked jealousy among some of the Jewish leaders, who opposed Paul and Barnabas and began to contradict their message (Acts 13:45). In response to this opposition, Paul and Barnabas boldly declared that they would turn to the Gentiles, quoting Isaiah 49:6: "I have made you a light for the Gentiles, that you may bring salvation to the ends of the earth" (Acts 13:47). This marked a pivotal moment in Paul's ministry, as he increasingly focused on spreading the Gospel to the Gentiles. While many Gentiles in Pisidian Antioch embraced the message with joy, the opposition from Jewish leaders intensified, leading to Paul and Barnabas being expelled from the city (Acts 13:50).

Iconium, Lystra, and Derbe – Healing and Persecution (Acts 14:1-20)

Undeterred by their expulsion from Pisidian Antioch, Paul and Barnabas traveled to Iconium, another significant city in Asia Minor. In Iconium, they again began their ministry in the synagogue, where their preaching resulted in a large number of both Jews and Gentiles coming to faith (Acts 14:1). However, their success also stirred up opposition from some Jews who poisoned the minds of the Gentiles against them (Acts 14:2). Despite this, Paul and Barnabas stayed in Iconium for a considerable time, boldly speaking for the Lord, who confirmed their message by enabling them to perform signs and wonders (Acts 14:3).

The situation in Iconium eventually became dangerous as the city became divided, with some siding with the apostles and others with their opponents. A plot to mistreat and stone Paul and Barnabas forced them to flee to the cities of Lystra and Derbe in Lycaonia (Acts 14:5-6). In

Lystra, Paul healed a man who had been lame from birth, a miracle that astonished the crowd. The people of Lystra, unfamiliar with Jewish monotheism, interpreted the miracle as a sign that Paul and Barnabas were gods in human form, calling them Hermes and Zeus and attempting to offer sacrifices to them (Acts 14:11-13).

Paul and Barnabas were horrified by this misunderstanding and urgently tried to redirect the people's worship toward the living God who made heaven and earth (Acts 14:15). Despite their efforts, the situation quickly deteriorated when Jews from Antioch and Iconium arrived and incited the crowd against Paul. The same people who had been ready to worship him as a god now turned against him, stoning him and leaving him for dead outside the city. Miraculously, Paul survived the stoning and, with remarkable resilience, continued his missionary work, moving on to Derbe with Barnabas (Acts 14:19-20).

Return to Antioch – Reporting Success (Acts 14:21-28)

After preaching the Gospel in Derbe and making many disciples, Paul and Barnabas decided to retrace their steps, revisiting the cities where they had established churches. They returned to Lystra, Iconium, and Pisidian Antioch, encouraging the believers to remain steadfast in the faith despite the hardships they had witnessed (Acts 14:21-22). Paul and Barnabas also appointed elders in each church, ensuring that the new Christian communities would have strong, local leadership to guide them (Acts 14:23).

Finally, Paul and Barnabas returned to Antioch in Syria, the church that had initially commissioned them for their missionary journey. Upon their arrival, they gathered the church together and reported all that God had done through them, particularly how He had opened a door of faith to the Gentiles (Acts 14:27). Their report was a testament to the success of their mission, despite the challenges and persecutions they had faced. The church in Antioch rejoiced in the work of God and the expansion of the Gospel.

Challenges and Successes

Paul's first missionary journey was a transformative period in the early Christian movement, marked by a mixture of challenges and successes. Paul and Barnabas encountered significant opposition and persecution, particularly from Jewish leaders who were resistant to their message. Yet, they also witnessed the powerful spread of the Gospel, with many Gentiles embracing the faith. The journey not only expanded the geographical reach of Christianity but also solidified Paul's role as the Apostle to the Gentiles. His experiences during this journey laid the groundwork for his subsequent missions and his enduring commitment to spreading the message of Christ to the farthest reaches of the Roman world.

In the chapters that follow, we will continue to trace Paul's missionary journeys, exploring his interactions with diverse communities, his teachings, and the growth of the early Christian Church. Through his perseverance, theological insights, and unwavering faith, Paul's legacy as one of the most influential figures in Christian history continues to inspire believers around the world.

CHAPTER 06

THE JERUSALEM COUNCIL

Paul's Visit to Jerusalem and the Decision on Gentile Inclusion

The Jerusalem Council, as recounted in Acts 15, stands as a watershed moment in the history of the early Christian Church. This assembly of apostolic leaders was convened to address a pressing theological and practical issue: whether Gentile converts to Christianity were required to observe Jewish customs, particularly circumcision, as a prerequisite for inclusion in the Christian community. The outcome of this council not only shaped the future of the

Church but also solidified the doctrinal foundation that would guide its growth as a universal faith.

Background and Context (Acts 15:1-5)

The inclusion of Gentiles in the Christian community had become a contentious issue as the Gospel spread beyond Jewish boundaries. The primary point of contention was whether Gentile converts needed to be circumcised and adhere to the Mosaic Law to be fully accepted as members of the Church. Certain Jewish Christians, often referred to as "Judaizers," insisted that the observance of Jewish customs was essential for salvation. This group believed that the covenantal sign of circumcision, which had been given to Abraham (Genesis 17:10-14), was still binding on all who wished to belong to God's people.

This insistence on circumcision led to a significant dispute between Paul and Barnabas and the Judaizers. Paul, who had been actively preaching to Gentiles and witnessing their conversion through faith in Christ, strongly opposed the imposition of Jewish law on Gentile believers. The church in Antioch, where the controversy was particularly intense, decided to send Paul and Barnabas, along with other representatives, to Jerusalem to seek a resolution from the apostles and elders.

The Council Begins (Acts 15:6-21)

Upon arriving in Jerusalem, Paul and Barnabas were welcomed by the Church, and they began to report on the success of their missionary efforts among the Gentiles. The apostles and elders convened to discuss the matter, recognizing the gravity of the issue. This meeting brought together leaders from different backgrounds: those who, like Peter and James, were rooted in Jewish tradition and had originally embraced the Gospel as faithful Jews, and those, like Paul and Barnabas, who had been reaching out to Gentiles with the message that faith in Christ alone was sufficient for salvation.

The debate was intense, with the Judaizers arguing that Gentiles must be circumcised and follow the Law of Moses to be saved (Acts 15:5). This position reflected a deep-seated belief in the necessity of the Law as the guide to righteous living and covenantal faithfulness. However, it also raised the critical question of whether the new covenant in Christ required adherence to the old covenant's ceremonial laws.

Peter's Testimony and Defense of Gentile Inclusion (Acts 15:7-11)

Peter, one of the foremost apostles and a respected leader in the Jerusalem Church, took the floor to offer his testimony. Recalling his own experience with Cornelius, a Gentile centurion whose household had received the Holy

Spirit without being circumcised (Acts 10), Peter argued that God had already shown His acceptance of Gentiles by giving them the Holy Spirit just as He had to Jewish believers. Peter stated, "God, who knows the heart, showed that he accepted them by giving the Holy Spirit to them, just as he did to us" (Acts 15:8).

Peter then questioned the wisdom of imposing the Jewish law on Gentile converts, describing it as a "yoke" that neither the current generation of Jews nor their ancestors had been able to bear. He boldly declared that both Jews and Gentiles are saved by the grace of the Lord Jesus Christ, not by the works of the Law (Acts 15:10-11). Peter's testimony was crucial in shifting the perspective of the assembly, highlighting that salvation was through faith in Christ alone—a principle that would become a cornerstone of Christian doctrine.

Paul and Barnabas's Report (Acts 15:12)

Following Peter's speech, Paul and Barnabas shared their experiences from their missionary journeys, recounting the signs and wonders God had performed among the Gentiles. Their testimony provided further evidence that God was at work among the Gentiles without requiring them to observe Jewish customs. The assembly listened in silence, recognizing that the inclusion of Gentiles was a divine initiative, not merely a human decision.

James's Judgment and the Council's Decision (Acts 15:13-21)

James, the brother of Jesus and a leading figure in the Jerusalem Church, then addressed the assembly. Known for his piety and deep respect for the Jewish tradition, James carried significant weight in the decision-making process. He began by affirming Peter's testimony and then referred to the words of the prophets, particularly Amos 9:11-12, which spoke of the restoration of David's fallen tent and the inclusion of the Gentiles in God's plan. James interpreted this prophecy as being fulfilled in the events they were witnessing, where God was calling a people for His name from among the Gentiles (Acts 15:14-18).

James proposed a solution that sought to respect both Jewish and Gentile believers. He suggested that Gentiles should not be burdened with the full weight of the Mosaic Law, particularly circumcision, but should be asked to abstain from certain practices that were particularly offensive to Jewish sensibilities and that were associated with idolatry and immorality. Specifically, he recommended that Gentiles abstain from food sacrificed to idols, from blood, from the meat of strangled animals, and from sexual immorality (Acts 15:20). These stipulations were meant to foster peace and unity within the diverse Christian community while upholding certain moral standards.

The Outcome and Impact of the Jerusalem Council

The decision of the Jerusalem Council was a pivotal moment in the history of Christianity. It clarified a fundamental doctrinal issue: that salvation is by grace through faith in Christ alone, without the necessity of adhering to Jewish customs. This decision aligned with Paul's teachings and provided a theological foundation that would support the Church's mission to the Gentiles.

1. Clarification of Doctrine: The council's ruling affirmed that Gentiles were not required to be circumcised or to follow the Mosaic Law to be saved. This was a monumental decision that reinforced the doctrine of justification by faith, a key tenet of Paul's theology, as expressed in his letters to the Romans and Galatians (Romans 3:28; Galatians 2:16). The council's conclusion that faith in Christ was sufficient for salvation helped to establish the theological basis for Christian liberty and the universality of the Gospel.

2. Unity in Diversity: The Jerusalem Council demonstrated the early Church's commitment to being a unified community that could embrace both Jewish and Gentile believers without imposing divisive cultural or religious barriers. The decision allowed for diversity within

the Church, where Jewish Christians could continue to observe their traditions while Gentile Christians were free from the obligations of the Law. This inclusivity set a precedent for how the Church would navigate cultural differences in the future.

3. Avoidance of Division: By addressing the issue of Gentile inclusion decisively, the council prevented what could have been a significant schism within the early Church. A division between Jewish and Gentile Christians could have severely weakened the Church's ability to spread the Gospel and might have led to the formation of separate, competing movements. The council's decision preserved the unity of the Church and allowed it to continue its mission with a clear and consistent message.

4. Witness to the World: The outcome of the Jerusalem Council sent a powerful message to the broader world: the Gospel of Jesus Christ transcended cultural and ethnic boundaries and was accessible to all people, regardless of their background. This inclusivity was a revolutionary concept in a world where religious identity was often closely tied to ethnicity and culture. The decision likely contributed to the rapid growth of Christianity among Gentiles and solidified its status as a universal faith.

Paul's visit to Jerusalem and the decisions made at the Jerusalem Council were pivotal in shaping the early Christian

Church. The council's resolution of the issue of Gentile inclusion affirmed the sufficiency of faith in Christ for salvation, promoted unity among diverse believers, and laid the groundwork for the Church's expansion into the Gentile world. The theological clarity and inclusive spirit that emerged from the Jerusalem Council continue to influence Christian thought and practice to this day, reflecting the Church's commitment to being a community of faith that transcends cultural and ethnic divisions.

CHAPTER 07

SECOND AND THIRD MISSIONARY JOURNEYS

Paul's Extensive Travels through Greece, Asia Minor, and Beyond

The Apostle Paul's second and third missionary journeys were marked by extensive travels, the establishment of numerous Christian communities, and the significant expansion of Christianity throughout the Roman Empire. These journeys illustrate Paul's relentless commitment to spreading the Gospel, even in the face of considerable opposition and hardship. His efforts during these journeys laid the foundation for the spread of Christianity in regions that would become central to the faith's development.

Second Missionary Journey (Acts 15:36 - 18:22)

Reuniting with Silas and Departure: Following the Jerusalem Council, Paul expressed a desire to revisit the churches he had established during his first missionary journey. His concern was for the spiritual well-being and growth of these early Christian communities (Acts 15:36). To accompany him, Paul chose Silas, a leader in the Jerusalem church who had proven himself a reliable partner in ministry (Acts 15:40). This decision marked the beginning of Paul's second missionary journey, which would take him through the regions of Phrygia and Galatia, and eventually into Europe.

Phrygia and Galatia: Paul and Silas traveled through Phrygia and Galatia, regions in Asia Minor where Paul had previously established churches (Acts 16:6). The purpose of this visit was to strengthen the believers, encourage them in their faith, and ensure that the teachings they had received were being faithfully followed. Paul's deep pastoral concern for these churches is evident in his letters, such as in Galatians, where he addresses issues of legalism and reaffirms the doctrine of justification by faith (Galatians 3:1-14).

The Macedonian Call (Acts 16:6-10): As Paul and Silas journeyed through Asia Minor, the Holy Spirit prevented them from preaching in certain areas, redirecting their mission toward new fields of labor. In a vision, Paul saw a man from Macedonia pleading, "Come over to Macedonia and help us" (Acts 16:9). Interpreting this as a divine call, Paul and his companions immediately set out for Macedonia, thus bringing the Gospel to Europe for the first time. This pivotal moment underscored the importance of divine guidance in Paul's missionary endeavors and expanded the geographical reach of the early Christian movement.

Philippi Conversion and Persecution: Upon arriving in Philippi, a leading city of Macedonia, Paul and Silas sought out a place of prayer by the river, where they encountered Lydia, a seller of purple cloth. Lydia, a Gentile worshiper of God, responded to Paul's message and, along with her household, was baptized (Acts 16:13-15). This conversion marked the establishment of the first Christian community in Europe. However, Paul's mission in Philippi was not without challenges. After Paul cast out a spirit of divination from a slave girl, her owners, enraged by the loss of their income, dragged Paul and Silas before the authorities. They were beaten, imprisoned, and placed in stocks (Acts 16:16-24). Despite their suffering, Paul and Silas prayed and sang hymns in prison, and an earthquake miraculously opened the prison doors. The jailer, witnessing these events, asked, "What must I do to be saved?" and, upon hearing the Gospel, he and his household were baptized (Acts 16:25-34). This incident highlights the power of the Gospel to bring salvation in the midst of persecution.

Thessalonica and Berea – Mixed Responses: From Philippi, Paul and Silas traveled to Thessalonica, where Paul preached in the synagogue for three Sabbaths, explaining and proving that the Messiah had to suffer and rise from the dead, and declaring that "This Jesus I am proclaiming to you is the Messiah" (Acts 17:1-3). While some Jews and a large number of God-fearing Greeks were persuaded, others, motivated by jealousy, stirred up a mob against Paul and Silas, forcing them to flee to Berea (Acts 17:5-10). In Berea, Paul found a more receptive audience; the Bereans were commended for their eagerness to examine the Scriptures daily to verify Paul's teachings (Acts 17:11). However, opposition from Thessalonica soon followed, and Paul was again forced to leave, this time heading toward Athens.

Athens – Engaging with Greek Philosophy: In Athens, Paul's spirit was provoked by the city's pervasive idolatry. He engaged with both Jews and God-fearing Gentiles in the synagogue, and with the local philosophers in the marketplace, eventually being invited to speak at the Areopagus, a prominent center of philosophical discussion (Acts 17:16-19). Here, Paul delivered one of his most famous sermons, using an altar inscribed "To an unknown god" as a starting point to introduce the Athenians to the one true God, the Creator of all things (Acts 17:22-31). He spoke of God's sovereignty, the futility of idolatry, and the resurrection of Jesus, which provoked mixed reactions. Some mocked the idea of resurrection, while others expressed interest in hearing more. Although only a few converts were recorded, including Dionysius the Areopagite and a woman named Damaris (Acts 17:32-34), Paul's time in Athens demonstrated his ability to contextualize the Gospel for different audiences.

Corinth – Establishing a Strong Christian Community: Paul's journey continued to Corinth, a bustling and morally corrupt city known for its commercial significance and licentiousness. Here, Paul met Aquila and Priscilla, Jewish tentmakers who had recently been expelled from Rome (Acts 18:1-3). Paul stayed with them and worked alongside them, using their home as a base for his ministry. Every Sabbath, Paul reasoned in the synagogue, trying to persuade both Jews and Greeks. Despite opposition from some Jews, Paul had a fruitful ministry in Corinth, staying there for a year and a half and establishing a strong Christian community (Acts 18:4-11). The Lord appeared to Paul in a vision, encouraging him not to be afraid, for He had "many people in this city" (Acts 18:9-10). This assurance strengthened Paul, and Corinth became a significant center of early Christianity, later receiving two of Paul's most important epistles, 1 and 2 Corinthians.

Third Missionary Journey (Acts 18:23 - 21:16)

Revisiting Previous Churches: Paul's third missionary journey began with a return to the regions of Galatia and Phrygia, where he had previously established churches (Acts 18:23). His purpose was to strengthen the disciples, ensuring that the believers continued to grow in their faith and remain steadfast in the teachings they had received. Paul's commitment to nurturing these early Christian communities is evident in his letters, where he frequently expresses concern for their spiritual health and unity (e.g., Galatians 1:6-9; 1 Corinthians 1:10-13).

Ephesus – A Major Center for Paul's Ministry: Paul then traveled to Ephesus, one of the most significant cities in Asia Minor, both in terms of size and cultural influence. Ephesus was known for the Temple of Artemis, one of the Seven Wonders of the Ancient World, and was a major hub of pagan worship and commerce. Paul spent an extended period of about two to three years in Ephesus, making it one of the most important centers of his ministry (Acts 19:1-10). During his time there, Paul performed many miracles, such as healing the sick and casting out evil spirits, which led to a widespread acknowledgment of the power of the name of

Jesus (Acts 19:11-12). These extraordinary events led many to abandon their magical practices, as demonstrated by the public burning of scrolls related to sorcery, valued at a significant sum of money (Acts 19:18-19). The growth of the Christian community in Ephesus, however, also led to conflict with those whose livelihoods depended on the worship of Artemis.

Conflict and Riots in Ephesus: The success of Paul's ministry in Ephesus threatened the local economy, particularly the business of silversmiths who made shrines of Artemis. A silversmith named Demetrius, concerned about the loss of income and the diminishing honor of Artemis, incited a large-scale riot against Paul and his companions (Acts 19:23-41). The riot highlighted the broader societal and economic implications of the spread of Christianity, as it challenged not only religious beliefs but also established economic practices. Paul was eventually persuaded by his disciples not to confront the angry mob, and the city clerk managed to calm the situation, allowing Paul to leave Ephesus and continue his journey.

Macedonia and Greece – Strengthening the Churches: After leaving Ephesus, Paul traveled through Macedonia, visiting the churches in Philippi, Thessalonica, and Berea, strengthening the believers and encouraging them in their faith (Acts 20:1-2). He then spent three months in Greece, likely in Corinth, where he wrote the Epistle to the Romans, one of his most theologically profound letters. In Romans, Paul elaborates on key doctrines such as justification by faith, the role of the Law, and the sovereignty of God in salvation history (Romans 3:21-31; Romans 9-11). Paul also took the opportunity to collect contributions from the Gentile churches for the poor believers in Jerusalem, demonstrating his concern for the unity and mutual support of the Christian community (Romans 15:25-27; 2 Corinthians 8-9).

Return to Jerusalem – A Foreseen Danger: Despite repeated warnings from fellow believers about the dangers awaiting him, Paul felt compelled by the Holy Spirit to return to Jerusalem (Acts 20:22-23). On his way back, Paul visited several cities, including Troas, where he revived a young man named Eutychus who had fallen asleep and died after falling from a window during one of Paul's lengthy sermons (Acts 20:7-12). Paul's journey to Jerusalem was marked by a deep sense of impending suffering, but also by a steadfast resolve to fulfill his mission, regardless of the personal cost. When he met with the elders of the Ephesian church in Miletus, Paul delivered an emotional farewell speech, warning them to be vigilant against false teachers and exhorting them to shepherd the church of God faithfully (Acts 20:17-38). Paul's determination to return to Jerusalem, even in the face of likely arrest and persecution, underscored his unwavering commitment to his calling and to the unity of the Church.

Paul's second and third missionary journeys covered vast geographical regions, including Greece, Asia Minor, and beyond. These journeys were characterized by the establishment of new Christian communities, the strengthening of existing ones, and the significant spread of Christianity into diverse cultural contexts. Paul's travels and teachings had a profound and lasting impact on the development of early Christianity, as he navigated cultural, religious, and economic challenges to proclaim the Gospel. His letters, written during these journeys, continue to provide foundational theological insights and practical guidance for Christian living. Despite facing intense opposition, persecution, and personal suffering, Paul's dedication to his mission remained steadfast, and his legacy as one of the greatest apostles and missionaries in Christian history endures to this day.

CHAPTER 08

THE EPISTLES TO THE THESSALONIANS

An In-Depth Exploration of Paul's Letters to the Thessalonians

The two Epistles to the Thessalonians, 1 Thessalonians and 2 Thessalonians, are among the earliest of Paul's writings and offer significant insights into his teachings on eschatology (the study of end times) and Christian living. These letters were addressed to the Christian community in Thessalonica, a prominent city in Greece, where Paul had established a church during his second missionary journey. Written in response to specific concerns and challenges faced by the Thessalonian believers, these letters provide a window into Paul's pastoral heart and theological depth.

1 Thessalonians: Encouragement and Eschatological Hope

Eschatological Themes and the Hope of Resurrection: One of the central themes of 1 Thessalonians is eschatology, particularly the concern about believers who had died before the anticipated return of Christ. The Thessalonians were anxious that those who had passed away might miss out on the blessings of Christ's return. In response, Paul provides comforting and clarifying teachings. In 1 Thessalonians 4:13-18, he assures them that "the dead in Christ will rise first," and that "we who are alive, who are left, will be caught up together with them in the clouds to meet the Lord in the air." This passage is one of the earliest and clearest references to what is often termed the "rapture" in Christian theology. Paul's message emphasizes the hope of resurrection and the ultimate reunion of all believers with Christ. His teaching here draws on Jewish apocalyptic traditions and reinterprets them in the light of the resurrection of Jesus, offering a profound sense of hope and assurance.

Christian Living and Ethical Exhortations: Alongside his eschatological teachings, Paul provides practical guidance on Christian living. He urges the Thessalonian believers to "live in a way that pleases God," as they had been taught (1

Thessalonians 4:1). This includes instructions on maintaining sexual purity, which was especially pertinent in a Greco-Roman context where sexual immorality was widespread. Paul's exhortation to "control your own body in holiness and honor" (1 Thessalonians 4:4) reflects the high ethical standards expected of Christians, who were to live in a manner that reflected their new identity in Christ. Additionally, Paul stresses the importance of brotherly love and a strong work ethic, encouraging believers to "aspire to live quietly, and to mind your own affairs, and to work with your hands" (1 Thessalonians 4:11). These instructions were aimed at fostering a community that was both self-sufficient and an example to outsiders.

The Day of the Lord: Another key eschatological theme in 1 Thessalonians is the "day of the Lord," a concept rooted in Old Testament prophecy (e.g., Amos 5:18-20; Joel 2:1-2) and associated with divine judgment and salvation. Paul warns that this day will come "like a thief in the night" (1 Thessalonians 5:2), emphasizing the unpredictability of Christ's return. He exhorts the Thessalonians to be vigilant and sober, living as "children of light and children of the day" (1 Thessalonians 5:5), in contrast to those who live in spiritual darkness. Paul's call for watchfulness is not merely about avoiding complacency but about embodying a lifestyle that reflects the imminent and transformative return of Christ.

2 Thessalonians: Clarification and Reinforcement

Eschatological Clarification: In 2 Thessalonians, Paul revisits and further clarifies his eschatological teachings. It appears that some in the Thessalonian community had misunderstood or been misled into thinking that "the day of the Lord" had already arrived (2 Thessalonians 2:2). This misunderstanding had caused confusion and concern. Paul corrects this by explaining that certain events must precede Christ's return, including the "rebellion" and the revelation of the "man of lawlessness" (2 Thessalonians 2:3-4). The "man of lawlessness" is often interpreted as an antichrist figure, a person or force that opposes God and exalts himself in the temple of God. Paul's description here is apocalyptic in nature, drawing from Jewish eschatological traditions while also reflecting the persecution and challenges faced by the early Church. Paul reassures the Thessalonians that these events will unfold according to God's sovereign plan, and that the ultimate victory belongs to Christ, who will "kill [the man of lawlessness] with the breath of his mouth" (2 Thessalonians 2:8).

Perseverance Amidst Persecution: A major concern for the Thessalonians was the persecution they were enduring. Paul acknowledges their suffering and encourages them to stand firm in their faith. He commends their faith and love, which have grown despite adversity (2 Thessalonians 1:3-4). Paul reminds them that God is just and will repay with affliction those who afflict them, while granting relief to the afflicted when Christ is revealed (2 Thessalonians 1:6-7). This dual theme of divine justice and eschatological hope is intended to fortify the Thessalonians against the trials they face, assuring them that their perseverance is not in vain.

Exhortation Against Idleness: In 2 Thessalonians, Paul also addresses the issue of idleness, which had become a problem within the community. Some believers, perhaps influenced by the belief that Christ's return was imminent, had stopped working and were relying on others for their sustenance. Paul strongly admonishes this behavior, stating, "If anyone is not willing to work, let him not eat" (2 Thessalonians 3:10). He urges the community to avoid those who are idle and disruptive, and to continue in the tradition of hard work that he himself modeled (2 Thessalonians 3:6-12). This exhortation reflects Paul's broader concern for order and discipline within the Christian community, as well as his emphasis on the dignity of labor.

Key Themes in Both Epistles

Eschatology: Both letters emphasize eschatological themes, particularly the return of Christ and the events surrounding it. Paul's teachings offer comfort and encouragement, assuring believers of their future hope and the ultimate triumph of Christ. His detailed eschatological instructions aim to correct misunderstandings and provide a theological framework that would sustain the Thessalonian believers through periods of uncertainty and persecution.

Christian Living: Paul's instructions on Christian conduct are central to both epistles. He exhorts the Thessalonians to live in a manner that reflects their faith in Christ, emphasizing love, sexual purity, and diligence. Paul's ethical teachings are grounded in the belief that Christians are called to be distinct from the surrounding culture, embodying the values of the Kingdom of God in their daily lives.

Perseverance and Endurance: The theme of perseverance runs through both letters, as Paul encourages the Thessalonians to remain steadfast in their faith despite external pressures. He acknowledges the reality of suffering and persecution but frames it within the context of eschatological hope, reminding the believers that their endurance will be rewarded when Christ returns.

Prayer and Watchfulness: Paul underscores the importance of prayer and vigilance, recognizing the unpredictability of Christ's return and the need for spiritual readiness. He urges the Thessalonians to be constant in prayer, to "pray without ceasing" (1 Thessalonians 5:17), and to remain alert, living as people who are fully aware of the times in which they live.

The Epistles to the Thessalonians offer a rich tapestry of theological insights and practical advice, reflecting Paul's deep concern for the spiritual well-being of the early Christian communities. Through these letters, Paul addresses both the doctrinal questions related to eschatology and the ethical challenges of Christian living. His teachings on the return of Christ, the resurrection, and the need for perseverance remain foundational to Christian eschatology. Moreover, Paul's pastoral care is evident in his exhortations to live in holiness, love, and readiness for the Lord's return. These letters continue to inspire and guide Christians today, providing timeless wisdom on how to live faithfully in anticipation of Christ's glorious return.

CHAPTER 09

THE CORINTHIAN CORRESPONDENCE

Paul's Letters to the Corinthians: A Comprehensive Exploration

The Corinthian Correspondence, comprising 1 Corinthians and 2 Corinthians, provides a profound glimpse into the challenges, controversies, and pastoral concerns that the Apostle Paul faced while shepherding the early Christian community in Corinth. These letters reveal the complexities of maintaining unity, holiness, and doctrinal integrity within a diverse and often morally challenging urban setting.

1 Corinthians: Addressing Division, Morality, and Doctrine

Background and Context

Paul wrote 1 Corinthians from Ephesus around AD 54-55 in response to troubling reports he had received about the Corinthian church. The reports came from members of Chloe's household (1 Corinthians 1:11) and a letter from the Corinthians themselves (1 Corinthians 7:1), highlighting various issues that were causing division and confusion within the community. Corinth, a major cosmopolitan city in the Roman Empire, was known for its wealth, diverse population, and moral laxity. The church in Corinth reflected these social dynamics, struggling with internal divisions, immorality, and misunderstandings about key aspects of Christian doctrine and practice.

Key Themes and Content

Unity in the Body of Christ: One of the most pressing issues Paul addresses in 1 Corinthians is the division within the church. The Corinthian believers had split into factions, each claiming allegiance to different leaders—Paul, Apollos, Cephas (Peter), or Christ (1 Corinthians 1:12). Paul vehemently opposes this division, reminding them that Christ is not divided and that they were all baptized into one body (1 Corinthians 1:13-17). Using the metaphor of the body, Paul emphasizes that the church is a single entity made up of many parts, each with a unique function but all interdependent (1

Corinthians 12:12-27). This teaching underscores the necessity of unity and mutual respect among believers, regardless of their gifts or social status.

Immorality and the Call to Holiness: Paul confronts serious moral lapses within the Corinthian church, most notably a case of incest where a man is living with his father's wife (1 Corinthians 5:1). Paul's response is stern; he calls for the expulsion of the unrepentant sinner to protect the integrity of the church and to encourage repentance (1 Corinthians 5:5-6). This incident illustrates Paul's commitment to maintaining holiness within the Christian community. He also addresses other issues related to sexual immorality, urging the Corinthians to flee from sexual sin and to honor God with their bodies, which are temples of the Holy Spirit (1 Corinthians 6:18-20). Paul's teaching here reflects a broader concern for the sanctity of the body and the moral purity of believers in a city known for its licentiousness.

Marriage, Celibacy, and Christian Freedom: In response to questions posed by the Corinthians, Paul provides guidance on marriage, celibacy, and the use of Christian freedom (1 Corinthians 7). He acknowledges that marriage is good and honorable but also extols the virtues of celibacy for those who can accept it, as it allows for undivided devotion to the Lord (1 Corinthians 7:32-35). Paul's nuanced approach to these issues highlights his pastoral sensitivity and his understanding of the diverse circumstances of his audience. He also discusses the use of Christian freedom, particularly in relation to eating food sacrificed to idols, advising that believers should be guided by love and the conscience of others, even if they have the knowledge that such idols are nothing (1 Corinthians 8:1-13).

Spiritual Gifts and the Primacy of Love (continued): The Corinthians' fascination with spiritual gifts had led to pride and disorder in the community, with some believers considering certain gifts—particularly speaking in tongues—as superior. Paul responds by emphasizing that all spiritual gifts are given by the same Spirit for the common good (1 Corinthians 12:4-7). He categorizes the various gifts, such as wisdom, knowledge, faith, healing, prophecy, and tongues, and asserts that each is necessary for the health of the body of Christ (1 Corinthians 12:8-11). Paul then presents the famous metaphor of the body, where every part, regardless of its perceived importance, is essential to the whole (1 Corinthians 12:12-27).

Paul's discussion culminates in 1 Corinthians 13, often referred to as the "Love Chapter," where he declares that love (agape) is the greatest of all gifts. He argues that without love, all other gifts are meaningless: "If I speak in the tongues of men and of angels, but have not love, I am a noisy gong or a clanging cymbal" (1 Corinthians 13:1). Paul describes love as patient, kind, and enduring, qualities that reflect the character of Christ. He stresses that love must be the guiding principle in the exercise of all spiritual gifts, for it is the greatest gift and the ultimate fulfillment of the law.

The Doctrine of the Resurrection: A significant portion of 1 Corinthians is devoted to the doctrine of the resurrection, specifically in chapter 15. Paul addresses doubts and misconceptions among the Corinthians regarding the resurrection of the dead. He affirms the centrality of Christ's resurrection to the Christian faith, declaring, "If Christ has not been raised, your faith is futile; you are still in your sins" (1 Corinthians 15:17). Paul presents the resurrection as a historical fact, witnessed by many, including himself (1 Corinthians 15:3-8). He then explains the nature of the resurrection body, contrasting it with the natural body. The resurrection body, he asserts, will be imperishable, glorious, and powerful, fit for eternal life in the kingdom of God (1 Corinthians 15:42-49). Paul concludes with a triumphant declaration of victory over death, urging the Corinthians to stand firm in their faith and labor for the Lord, knowing that their work is not in vain (1 Corinthians 15:54-58).

2 Corinthians: Defense of Apostolic Authority and Pastoral Encouragement

Background and Context

2 Corinthians was written as a follow-up to the first letter, addressing ongoing challenges within the Corinthian church and defending Paul's apostolic authority. By the time Paul wrote this letter, his relationship with the Corinthians had become strained due to the influence of false apostles who questioned his legitimacy and sought to undermine his ministry. Paul's tone in 2 Corinthians is more personal and emotional, reflecting the depth of his concern for the Corinthian believers and the pain caused by their wavering loyalty.

Key Themes and Content

Comfort in Affliction and God's Strength in Weakness: Paul opens 2 Corinthians with a reflection on the comfort God provides in the midst of suffering (2 Corinthians 1:3-7). He shares his own experiences of affliction, describing the trials he faced in Asia that were so severe he "despaired of life itself" (2 Corinthians 1:8). Yet, Paul emphasizes that these experiences taught him to rely not on himself but on God, who raises the dead (2 Corinthians 1:9). This theme of God's strength being made perfect in weakness runs throughout the letter. In 2 Corinthians 12:7-10, Paul famously speaks of his "thorn in the flesh," a persistent affliction that kept him humble and dependent on God's grace. Despite pleading with the Lord to remove it,

Paul accepts the Lord's response: "My grace is sufficient for you, for my power is made perfect in weakness." This teaching offers profound comfort to believers, affirming that God's power is often most evident in our weaknesses and struggles.

The Collection for the Saints: Another significant theme in 2 Corinthians is Paul's ongoing effort to organize a collection for the poor believers in Jerusalem. Paul devotes two chapters (2 Corinthians 8-9) to encouraging the Corinthians to contribute generously to this cause. He presents giving as an act of grace and an expression of Christian love, urging the Corinthians to follow the example of the Macedonian churches, who gave generously despite their own poverty (2 Corinthians 8:1-5). Paul highlights the principles of generosity and equality, teaching that those who have more should help those who have less, so that there may be fairness (2 Corinthians 8:13-15). He also assures the Corinthians that their gifts will be administered with integrity and transparency (2 Corinthians 8:20-21). Paul's teaching on giving in these chapters remains a foundational text for Christian stewardship and charity.

Defense of Apostolic Authority: A major concern in 2 Corinthians is Paul's defense of his apostolic authority. His opponents, whom he sarcastically refers to as "super-apostles" (2 Corinthians 11:5; 12:11), had criticized Paul's appearance, speaking abilities, and credentials, attempting to undermine his influence in the Corinthian church. In response, Paul offers a robust defense of his ministry, highlighting his sincerity, integrity, and the hardships he endured for the sake of the Gospel (2 Corinthians 11:23-28). He contrasts his ministry with that of the false apostles, asserting that he preaches Christ with authenticity and not for personal gain (2 Corinthians 2:17; 4:2). Paul's defense reaches a climax in chapters 11 and 12, where he recounts his sufferings, visions, and the "thorn in the flesh," all of which demonstrate that his apostleship is marked by divine power, even in human weakness. He concludes by reaffirming his commitment to the Corinthians, despite their doubts, and by warning those who continue to challenge his authority (2 Corinthians 13:2-3).

Reconciliation and Forgiveness: In 2 Corinthians, Paul also addresses the need for reconciliation within the church, particularly concerning a repentant member who had been previously disciplined. Paul urges the Corinthians to forgive and comfort this individual, reaffirming their love for him so that he is not "overwhelmed by excessive sorrow" (2 Corinthians 2:7). This emphasis on forgiveness and restoration reflects Paul's pastoral concern for the spiritual well-being of all believers, as well as his understanding of the church as a community of grace. Paul's approach to church discipline balances the need for holiness with the call to mercy and reconciliation, aiming to restore rather than alienate.

Spiritual Warfare and the Power of God: Finally, Paul acknowledges the reality of spiritual warfare, urging the Corinthians to be vigilant against the schemes of Satan (2 Corinthians 2:11). In 2 Corinthians 10:3-5, Paul describes the nature of this warfare, stating that "the weapons of our warfare are not of the flesh but have divine power to destroy strongholds." He explains that this spiritual battle involves taking every thought captive to obey Christ and demolishing arguments and pretensions that set themselves against the knowledge of God. Paul's teaching on spiritual warfare underscores the importance of relying on God's power and truth in the face of opposition, both from within and outside the church.

Commentary and Analysis

The Corinthian Correspondence offers a rich and multifaceted exploration of early Christian life, theology, and pastoral care. Through these letters, Paul addresses a wide array of issues, ranging from doctrinal disputes to ethical challenges, reflecting the complexities of maintaining a vibrant Christian community in a morally and culturally diverse environment like Corinth.

Unity in Diversity: One of the most striking aspects of these letters is Paul's insistence on unity within the body of Christ, despite the diversity of its members. The Corinthians struggled with divisions based on loyalty to different leaders, social status, and the exercise of spiritual gifts. Paul's response, particularly in 1 Corinthians, emphasizes that unity is not about uniformity but about mutual respect, love, and the recognition that all believers are interconnected and equally valuable in the eyes of God.

The Challenge of Holiness in a Pagan Culture: Corinth was a city known for its wealth, sophistication, and moral decadence. The challenges faced by the Corinthian Christians in maintaining holiness amidst such an environment are evident throughout Paul's letters. His teachings on sexual purity, marriage, and the proper use of Christian freedom reflect his deep concern for the moral integrity of the church. Paul's call to holiness is not simply about following rules but about embodying the transformative power of the Gospel in everyday life.

The Centrality of the Resurrection: Paul's teaching on the resurrection in 1 Corinthians 15 is a theological high point, not only in the Corinthian Correspondence but in the New Testament as a whole. By affirming the bodily resurrection of believers, Paul provides a powerful counter to both the Greek philosophical disdain for the body and the doubts of some within the Corinthian church. The resurrection is presented as the cornerstone of Christian hope, with profound implications for how believers live and view their present and future existence.

Pastoral Sensitivity and Theological Depth: Throughout both letters, Paul demonstrates a remarkable balance between pastoral sensitivity and theological depth. He is deeply concerned for the spiritual welfare of the Corinthians, yet he does not shy away from confronting their errors and challenging them to grow in maturity. His teachings on love, forgiveness, generosity, and spiritual warfare are not only practical but are also deeply rooted in his understanding of the Gospel and the character of God.

The letters to the Corinthians remain some of the most influential writings in the New Testament, offering timeless wisdom on a wide range of issues that are still relevant to the church today. Paul's correspondence with the Corinthians reveals the challenges of living out the Christian faith in a complex and often hostile environment, while also showcasing the transformative power of the Gospel. His teachings on unity, holiness, love, and the resurrection continue to inspire and guide believers as they seek to live faithfully in the midst of a diverse and ever-changing world. The Corinthian Correspondence is a testament to Paul's enduring legacy as a pastor, theologian, and apostle to the early church.

93

CHAPTER 10

IMPRISONMENT AND THE PRISON EPISTLES

Paul's Imprisonment in Rome: A Pivotal Chapter in His Ministry

Paul's imprisonment in Rome represents a crucial and defining period in his life and ministry. While Paul was imprisoned multiple times throughout his missionary journeys, his Roman imprisonment, which likely occurred in the early 60s AD, holds particular significance both for the development of early Christianity and for the profound theological contributions that emerged during this time. Although the New Testament provides details of his arrest and journey to Rome, the exact circumstances and reasons for his imprisonment are complex and subject to various historical interpretations. Nevertheless, this period in Paul's life is marked by his unwavering commitment to the Gospel, his continued pastoral care for the churches, and the writing of several of his most influential letters.

Reasons for Imprisonment

The specific reasons for Paul's imprisonment in Rome are not explicitly detailed in the New Testament, but several contributing factors can be inferred from his earlier experiences and the political-religious climate of the time.

Preaching the Gospel: Paul's steadfast dedication to preaching the Gospel of Jesus Christ was a primary reason for the opposition he faced. His message, which proclaimed Jesus as the risen Lord and Savior, directly challenged both Jewish religious authorities and the Roman imperial cult. In the Roman Empire, where the emperor was often revered as a god, Paul's proclamation of Jesus as the only true Lord was subversive and potentially seditious. This challenge to the established religious and social order likely contributed to the hostility he encountered, both from local authorities and from Jewish leaders who saw his teachings as a threat to traditional Judaism.

Conflict with Jewish Authorities: Throughout his ministry, Paul had numerous confrontations with Jewish leaders who opposed his teachings, particularly his mission to the Gentiles and his rejection of the necessity of following the Mosaic Law for salvation. These conflicts often led to accusations against Paul, inciting crowds and causing disturbances. The Book of Acts records several instances where Jewish authorities sought to arrest or harm Paul, such as in Acts 21, where Paul was accused of bringing Gentiles into the temple and defiling it. This accusation led to a violent mob attack and ultimately to Paul's arrest by Roman authorities, who intervened to prevent a lynching.

Roman Citizenship: Paul's status as a Roman citizen played a dual role in his imprisonment. On one hand, it afforded him certain legal protections, such as the right to a fair trial and protection from summary execution. On the other hand, it also made him subject to Roman law and scrutiny. Roman officials, particularly those charged with maintaining public order, would have viewed Paul as a potential troublemaker, especially if his activities were seen as inciting unrest or challenging imperial authority. Paul's appeal to Caesar, a right he exercised as a Roman citizen (Acts 25:11), resulted in his transfer to Rome for trial, which eventually led to his prolonged house arrest.

Accusations in Jerusalem: The immediate cause of Paul's journey to Rome was his arrest in Jerusalem. Acts 21-26 provides a detailed account of the events leading to his arrest. Paul was accused by some Jews of bringing Gentiles into the temple, a charge that was both inflammatory and false. This accusation led to a riot, during which Paul was seized by the crowd and nearly killed. Rescued by Roman soldiers, Paul was eventually transferred to Caesarea, where he stood trial before various Roman officials, including Felix, Festus, and King Agrippa. After two years of imprisonment in Caesarea and facing the prospect of an unjust trial in Jerusalem, Paul appealed to Caesar, invoking his right as a Roman citizen to have his case heard by the emperor in Rome.

The Prison Epistles

During his imprisonment in Rome, Paul was not idle; instead, he continued to exercise his apostolic ministry through writing. This period gave rise to some of the most theologically rich and pastorally sensitive letters in the New Testament, collectively known as the "Prison Epistles." These include Ephesians, Philippians, Colossians, and Philemon. Despite his confinement, Paul's letters reflect deep spiritual insight, a profound sense of joy and hope, and a continued concern for the well-being of the Christian communities he had helped establish.

Ephesians: The Epistle to the Ephesians is notable for its emphasis on the unity and cosmic scope of the Church. Paul explores the "mystery" of God's plan, which was revealed through Christ and involves bringing together Jews and Gentiles into one body, the Church (Ephesians 2:11-22). The letter also discusses the spiritual blessings believers have in Christ, their identity as God's workmanship, and the importance of spiritual growth and maturity. Ephesians 6:10-18 contains the famous passage on the "armor of God," where Paul exhorts believers to stand firm against spiritual warfare by putting on the full armor provided by God. This epistle, with its lofty theological reflections and practical exhortations, underscores the importance of unity, holiness, and perseverance in the Christian life.

Philippians: Philippians is often described as Paul's "letter of joy," despite being written during a time of personal hardship. Throughout the letter, Paul repeatedly encourages the Philippians to "rejoice in the Lord" (Philippians 4:4) and to adopt the mindset of Christ, characterized by humility and selflessness (Philippians 2:5-11). Paul also reflects on his own circumstances, expressing contentment and confidence in Christ, regardless of his situation: "I have learned in whatever situation I am to be content" (Philippians 4:11). The letter highlights themes of joy, partnership in the Gospel, and the pursuit of spiritual goals, with Paul urging the Philippians to "press on toward the goal for the prize of the upward call of God in Christ Jesus" (Philippians 3:14). This epistle also includes personal expressions of gratitude for the support the Philippian church had provided to Paul, making it one of the most intimate and affectionate of Paul's letters.

Colossians: The Epistle to the Colossians addresses the supremacy of Christ and the sufficiency of His work for salvation. Paul combats false teachings that had infiltrated the church, likely involving elements of Jewish legalism, asceticism, and early Gnostic ideas. He emphasizes that Christ is "the image of the invisible God, the firstborn of all creation" (Colossians 1:15) and that "in him the whole fullness of deity dwells bodily" (Colossians 2:9). Paul exhorts the Colossians to remain rooted in Christ, rejecting any philosophy or tradition that detracts from the centrality of Christ's work on the cross. The letter also contains practical instructions for Christian living, including exhortations for households and advice on how believers should conduct themselves in their relationships and in society (Colossians 3:1-4:6). Colossians, therefore, serves as both a theological treatise on the person and work of Christ and a practical guide for living out the implications of this truth.

Philemon: The Epistle to Philemon is a personal letter, distinct from Paul's other prison writings due to its brevity and specific focus. It is addressed to Philemon, a wealthy Christian in Colossae, concerning Onesimus, a slave who had run away from Philemon, possibly after committing some offense. During Paul's imprisonment, Onesimus became a Christian, and Paul sends him back to Philemon with this letter, appealing for Onesimus to be received not as a slave but as a "beloved brother" in Christ (Philemon 1:16). Paul's letter is a powerful example of Christian reconciliation and the transformative power of the Gospel, as it challenges the social norms of the day and emphasizes the new identity and relationship that believers share in Christ.

Paul's Ministry During Imprisonment

Despite being confined, Paul's ministry continued to flourish. His imprisonment provided opportunities to witness to those around him, including members of the Roman guard and others who visited him (Philippians 1:12-14). Paul's letters during this time reflect a sense of divine purpose in his suffering, as he saw his chains as serving to advance the Gospel. His ability to write and send letters meant that he remained connected to the churches he had founded, offering guidance, encouragement, and correction as needed. Paul's writings from this period are characterized by a deep theological reflection, a pastoral concern for the unity and maturity of the Church, and a personal joy and contentment rooted in his relationship with Christ.

Paul's imprisonment in Rome marks a significant phase in his apostolic ministry, during which he continued to exert a profound influence on the early Christian Church through his writings. The Prison Epistles—Ephesians, Philippians, Colossians, and Philemon—are enduring testimonies to Paul's theological depth, pastoral heart, and unwavering commitment to the Gospel. These letters, written in the face of adversity, continue to inspire and guide Christians today, offering timeless truths about the nature of the Church, the supremacy of Christ, the joy of Christian fellowship, and the power of reconciliation. Paul's time in Rome, though marked by physical confinement, was a period of great spiritual productivity, leaving a legacy that has shaped the Christian faith for centuries.

CHAPTER 11

THE PASTORAL EPISTLES

Paul's Letters to Timothy and Titus: A Deep Dive into the Pastoral Epistles

The Pastoral Epistles, consisting of 1 Timothy, 2 Timothy, and Titus, are three New Testament letters written by the Apostle Paul to his trusted associates and fellow church leaders, Timothy and Titus. These letters are essential for understanding the early church's structure, leadership, and pastoral care. They offer guidance on how to maintain doctrinal purity, address false teachings, and ensure the spiritual health of the Christian communities they were overseeing.

Purpose of the Letters to Timothy and Titus

Pastoral Guidance: Paul's letters to Timothy and Titus were written to provide practical and theological guidance for their roles as church leaders. Timothy was stationed in Ephesus, a significant center of early Christianity, while Titus was serving in Crete, an island known for its challenging moral environment (Titus 1:12). Paul recognized the difficulties they faced and wrote to offer support and instructions on managing their congregations effectively.

Combatting False Teaching: One of the primary concerns in the Pastoral Epistles is the presence of false teachers who were spreading heresies within the early Christian communities. These false doctrines threatened the integrity of the Gospel message. Paul instructed Timothy and Titus to stand firm against these distortions, to teach sound doctrine, and to protect their congregations from being led astray (1 Timothy 1:3-7, Titus 1:10-16).

Appointing Church Leaders: Another key focus of these letters is the selection and appointment of church leaders. Paul provides detailed criteria for the qualifications of elders (also referred to as bishops or overseers) and deacons, emphasizing the importance of choosing leaders who are above reproach, spiritually mature, and capable of teaching and leading by example (1 Timothy 3:1-13, Titus 1:5-9).

Instruction on Church Conduct: Paul offers comprehensive guidance on how various members of the Christian community should conduct themselves. These instructions include directives on prayer, the role of women in worship, relationships with authorities, and the ethical behavior expected of believers. Paul's goal was to ensure that the Christian communities would reflect Christ's teachings in their daily lives and interactions (1 Timothy 2:1-15, Titus 2:1-10).

Key Lessons from the Pastoral Epistles

Church Leadership: The Pastoral Epistles underscore the critical importance of strong, qualified leadership within the church. Paul's criteria for church leaders focus on moral integrity, doctrinal soundness, and the ability to manage both their households and the church community effectively. These letters make it clear that the spiritual health of the church is closely tied to the character and competence of its leaders (1 Timothy 3:1-7, Titus 1:6-9).

Sound Doctrine: Throughout these letters, Paul emphasizes the need to uphold and teach sound doctrine. He warns against the dangers of false teachings, which can lead to divisions and spiritual decay within the church. Paul encourages Timothy and Titus to be diligent in teaching the truth of the Gospel and to correct those who deviate from it, ensuring that the faith handed down from the apostles remains uncorrupted (1 Timothy 4:1-6, Titus 2:1).

Pastoral Care: Paul's letters reveal his deep concern for the spiritual well-being of the believers under Timothy's and Titus's care. He advises them on how to approach various pastoral duties with compassion, patience, and wisdom. This includes offering correction when necessary, providing encouragement, and being examples of faith and godliness to their congregations (2 Timothy 2:24-26, Titus 2:7-8).

Personal Example and Endurance: Paul himself serves as a model for Timothy and Titus, especially in the areas of endurance and faithfulness. Despite facing persecution, imprisonment, and eventual martyrdom, Paul remained steadfast in his commitment to the Gospel. He encourages Timothy, in particular, to persevere in his ministry, to endure suffering, and to continue proclaiming the Gospel with the same dedication that Paul had demonstrated (2 Timothy 4:1-8).

Expository Overview of the Pastoral Epistles

1 Timothy: The first letter to Timothy provides extensive instructions on church organization and leadership. Paul addresses the qualifications for bishops and deacons, emphasizing the need for these leaders to be blameless, temperate, and capable of teaching (1 Timothy 3:1-13). He

also tackles issues such as false teachings, proper conduct in worship, and the care of widows (1 Timothy 5:1-16). Paul's instructions to Timothy are both practical and theological, guiding him in maintaining the integrity and order of the church in Ephesus.

2 Timothy: As Paul's final letter, 2 Timothy is deeply personal and reflective. Written during Paul's second imprisonment in Rome, it contains his last words of encouragement to Timothy. Paul reminds Timothy of his calling, urges him to "fan into flame the gift of God" (2 Timothy 1:6), and encourages him to endure hardship as a good soldier of Christ Jesus (2 Timothy 2:3). The letter also contains warnings about the difficult times ahead, including the spread of false teachings and moral decay (2 Timothy 3:1-9). Despite these challenges, Paul emphasizes the enduring power and value of Scripture, which is "breathed out by God and profitable for teaching, for reproof, for correction, and for training in righteousness" (2 Timothy 3:16). Paul's words convey a sense of urgency and a deep desire for Timothy to remain faithful to his ministry until the end.

Titus: The letter to Titus focuses on establishing order and sound doctrine in the church on the island of Crete. Paul instructs Titus to appoint elders in every town, ensuring that these leaders meet specific moral and spiritual qualifications (Titus 1:5-9). He also addresses the need to confront false teachers and to promote sound doctrine among different groups within the church, including older men, older women, young women, young men, and slaves (Titus 2:1-10). The letter emphasizes the importance of good works as evidence of a transformed life in Christ and highlights the transformative power of God's grace, which teaches believers to live "self-controlled, upright, and godly lives" (Titus 2:11-14).

The Pastoral Epistles offer a rich blend of theological instruction and practical advice, tailored to the specific challenges faced by Timothy and Titus in their respective ministries. Paul's concern for sound doctrine, effective leadership, and the spiritual health of the church is evident throughout these letters.

Theology of Leadership: Paul's teachings on church leadership are foundational for understanding the role of elders and deacons in the church. His emphasis on character and competence suggests that leadership in the church is not merely about holding a position of authority but about embodying the qualities of Christ and serving the community with humility and integrity. This theology of leadership continues to influence Christian thought on ministry and church governance.

Combatting False Doctrine: Paul's warnings against false teachings reflect the early church's struggle to maintain the purity of the Gospel in the face of various heresies. His insistence on sound doctrine underscores the importance of theological education and discernment for church leaders. Paul's approach to combating false doctrine is both proactive, through the teaching of truth, and reactive, through the correction of error.

Pastoral Care and Personal Example: The letters highlight the importance of pastoral care, not only in addressing the spiritual needs of the congregation but also in modeling Christian virtues. Paul's relationship with Timothy and Titus exemplifies the mentor-mentee dynamic, where experienced leaders invest in the next generation, providing them with the tools and encouragement they need to succeed in ministry. Paul's own example of perseverance in the face of trials serves as a powerful testament to the strength and endurance required in pastoral ministry.

Paul's letters to Timothy and Titus remain vital resources for understanding the early church's structure, leadership, and doctrinal integrity. The Pastoral Epistles provide timeless guidance for church leaders, emphasizing the importance of sound doctrine, moral integrity, and compassionate pastoral care. Through these letters, Paul's legacy as a mentor, pastor, and apostle continues to inspire and instruct church leaders today, offering a model of faithful ministry that is grounded in the teachings of Christ and the power of the Gospel.

CHAPTER 12

PAUL'S ARREST AND TRIAL

The Circumstances Leading to Paul's Arrest in Jerusalem: A Detailed Examination

Paul's arrest in Jerusalem marks a pivotal moment in his ministry, setting off a chain of events that would ultimately lead him to Rome. The narrative, as detailed in the Book of Acts, provides a comprehensive account of the factors and circumstances that culminated in his arrest, trials, and eventual journey to the heart of the Roman Empire. This period is crucial not only for understanding the final stages of Paul's life but also for recognizing the complexities of his mission and the intense opposition he faced.

Why Was Paul Sent to Rome?

Paul's journey to Rome was the direct result of his decision to appeal to Caesar, the highest authority in the Roman Empire. After his arrest in Jerusalem, Paul found himself entangled in a complex web of accusations and political maneuvering by Jewish leaders who were vehemently opposed to his teachings. Given the escalating threats to his life and the apparent bias of local authorities, Paul, as a Roman citizen, exercised his legal right to have his case heard by Caesar. This appeal set in motion the events that led to his transfer to Rome, where he would stand trial before the emperor himself. The decision to appeal to Caesar was not just a legal maneuver; it was a strategic move by Paul, reflecting his desire to spread the Gospel even in the heart of the empire, as well as to seek a fair trial beyond the reach of his accusers in Jerusalem (Acts 25:10-12).

Why Was Paul Arrested?

Paul's arrest in Jerusalem was the result of a series of events that highlighted the growing tension between his mission and the traditional Jewish authorities. The narrative in Acts provides a detailed account of the factors leading up to his arrest, which can be summarized as follows:

Arrival in Jerusalem: Paul's journey to Jerusalem was motivated by his desire to deliver a collection he had gathered from Gentile churches for the poor believers in Jerusalem (Romans 15:25-27, 1 Corinthians 16:1-4). Upon his arrival, Paul met with James and the elders of the Jerusalem church, who informed him about the concerns among Jewish believers regarding his teachings. They had heard rumors that Paul was teaching Jews living among the Gentiles to forsake the Law of Moses, which included not circumcising their children or following Jewish customs (Acts 21:20-21). To address these concerns and to demonstrate his respect for Jewish traditions, Paul agreed to participate in a purification ritual at the temple, which was intended to show his adherence to the Law (Acts 21:23-26).

Accusations by Jewish Leaders: Despite Paul's efforts to maintain peace, certain Jews from Asia (likely from Ephesus, where Paul had faced significant opposition) recognized him in the temple and stirred up a crowd against him. They falsely accused Paul of bringing Gentiles into the temple's inner courts, an area reserved exclusively for Jews. This accusation was serious, as it implied that Paul had defiled the holy place, which could incite severe punishment under Jewish law (Acts 21:27-29). The crowd, inflamed by these accusations, seized Paul and dragged him out of the temple, leading to a violent uproar.

Riot at the Temple and Arrest by Roman Authorities: The situation quickly escalated into a riot, drawing the attention of the Roman authorities stationed in Jerusalem to maintain order during the volatile times of Jewish festivals. The Roman commander, Claudius Lysias, intervened to prevent Paul from being lynched by the mob. Not fully understanding the nature of the accusations against Paul, the commander initially mistook him for an Egyptian rebel leader who had recently led a revolt (Acts 21:37-38). To restore order, Lysias ordered Paul to be bound with chains and taken into custody (Acts 21:31-33). This moment, marked by Paul's binding in chains, fulfilled the prophecy given to him earlier by the prophet Agabus, who had warned that Paul would be bound and delivered into the hands of the Gentiles if he went to Jerusalem (Acts 21:10-11).

The Outcome of Paul's Trial: A Series of Legal Proceedings

The series of events following Paul's arrest are meticulously documented in Acts 21-28, providing insight into the legal and political challenges Paul faced:

Trial Before the Sanhedrin (Acts 22-23): After his arrest, Paul was brought before the Jewish Sanhedrin, the highest Jewish religious court, to address the accusations against him. In his defense, Paul emphasized his background as a Pharisee and his strict adherence to Jewish law. Sensing the division within the Sanhedrin between Pharisees and

Sadducees, Paul cleverly declared his belief in the resurrection, a doctrine held by the Pharisees but rejected by the Sadducees (Acts 23:6-8). This statement caused a sharp dispute between the two factions, disrupting the proceedings. Fearing for Paul's safety due to the escalating violence, the Roman commander ordered him to be taken back to the barracks.

Transferred to Caesarea (Acts 23:23-24:27): Due to the increasing hostility and a plot by some Jews to assassinate Paul, the Roman commander decided to transfer Paul to Caesarea, the provincial capital, where he would stand trial before the Roman governor Felix. This transfer, conducted under heavy guard, highlighted the seriousness of the threats against Paul. In Caesarea, Paul faced a series of trials before governors Felix and later Festus, as well as a hearing before King Agrippa. During these trials, Paul defended himself against the charges brought by the Jewish leaders, consistently asserting his innocence and the continuity of his teachings with Jewish beliefs (Acts 24:10-21). However, despite the lack of evidence against him, Paul's case remained unresolved, partly due to the political complexities of the situation and Felix's hope for a bribe (Acts 24:26-27).

Appeal to Caesar (Acts 25): When Festus succeeded Felix as governor, the Jewish leaders renewed their accusations against Paul, seeking to have him transferred back to Jerusalem, where they planned to ambush and kill him

(Acts 25:1-3). Recognizing the danger and the likelihood of an unfair trial in Jerusalem, Paul exercised his right as a Roman citizen to appeal to Caesar (Acts 25:10-12). This appeal effectively removed his case from the jurisdiction of the local authorities and ensured that he would be sent to Rome for trial before the emperor. Festus, seeing no reason to deny the appeal, granted Paul's request, thus setting the stage for his journey to Rome.

Journey to Rome (Acts 27-28): Paul's journey to Rome was fraught with difficulties, including a perilous sea voyage and a shipwreck on the island of Malta (Acts 27:13-44). Despite these hardships, Paul continued to minister to those around him, performing miracles and sharing the Gospel even during the journey. After several months on Malta, Paul and his companions finally continued their journey to Rome, arriving after a long and arduous voyage (Acts 28:11-16).

Arrival in Rome (Acts 28): Upon arrival in Rome, Paul was placed under house arrest, where he was allowed to live in a rented house while awaiting his trial before Caesar. During this time, Paul continued his ministry, receiving visitors and preaching the Gospel "with all boldness and without hindrance" (Acts 28:30-31). Although the Book of Acts concludes with Paul still under house arrest, early church tradition suggests that Paul was eventually released from this first Roman imprisonment, continued his missionary work for a few more years, and was eventually rearrested and martyred under the emperor Nero.

Theological Reflections on Paul's Arrest and Trials

Paul's arrest and the subsequent trials underscore several key theological themes that are central to his life and ministry:

Sovereignty of God: Throughout the narrative, it is clear that Paul's arrest, trials, and eventual journey to Rome are not merely the result of human actions but are part of God's sovereign plan. Paul's decision to appeal to Caesar and his eventual arrival in Rome fulfilled his long-standing desire to preach the Gospel in the heart of the Roman Empire (Romans 1:15, Acts 23:11). Despite the opposition he faced, God's providence is evident in Paul's protection, his opportunities to witness before rulers and authorities, and the continuation of his ministry even under arrest.

Endurance in Suffering: Paul's experiences highlight the theme of endurance in the face of suffering and persecution. Throughout his trials, Paul remains steadfast in his faith and committed to his mission. His letters from this period, particularly those written from prison (the so-called "Prison Epistles"), reflect his deep trust in God and his belief that suffering for the sake of the Gospel is a privilege and a means of glorifying Christ (Philippians 1:12-14, 2 Timothy 2:8-10).

Witnessing Through Trials: Paul's trials provide a powerful example of how believers can bear witness to Christ even in the most challenging circumstances. Paul's defense before the Sanhedrin, his testimony before Felix, Festus, and Agrippa, and his interactions with those he encountered on his journey to Rome all served as opportunities to proclaim the Gospel. Paul's ability to articulate his faith clearly and boldly in these situations serves as a model for Christian witness under persecution.

The circumstances leading to Paul's arrest in Jerusalem and his subsequent journey to Rome are rich in historical and theological significance. These events, recorded in the Book of Acts, not only detail the legal and political challenges Paul faced but also highlight his unwavering commitment to his mission and his deep trust in God's sovereign plan. Paul's journey to Rome, driven by his appeal to Caesar, ultimately fulfilled his desire to preach the Gospel at the heart of the Roman Empire, and his experiences during this period continue to inspire believers to endure in their faith and to witness boldly for Christ, regardless of the circumstances.

CHAPTER 13

THE JOURNEY TO ROME

Paul's Voyage to Rome as a Prisoner: A Journey of Faith, Adversity, and Divine Providence

Paul's journey to Rome as a prisoner, recounted in Acts 27-28, stands as one of the most dramatic and theologically rich narratives in the New Testament. This journey, filled with peril, divine intervention, and ultimately the fulfillment of God's plan, not only underscores Paul's unwavering faith but also serves as a powerful demonstration of God's sovereignty and protection over His servants.

Setting Sail: The Beginning of a Perilous Journey (Acts 27:1-8)

The journey began when Paul, along with other prisoners, was placed under the custody of a Roman centurion named Julius, a member of the Imperial Regiment. Their departure from Caesarea marked the start of a voyage that would take them across the eastern Mediterranean towards Rome. The ship they initially boarded sailed along the coastline of Asia Minor, making slow progress due to unfavorable winds (Acts 27:4-5). The decision to sail during the late autumn, a period known for its treacherous seas, added to the inherent risks of the voyage. The narrative provides a vivid depiction of the challenges faced by ancient mariners, highlighting the difficulties of navigating in a region where sudden storms could easily arise, turning the journey into a life-threatening ordeal.

Challenges at Sea: A Test of Faith and Leadership (Acts 27:9-20)

As they continued their voyage, the ship faced increasing challenges, including adverse winds that forced them to change course and seek shelter along the southern coast of Crete (Acts 27:7-8). The situation became increasingly precarious as they approached the treacherous waters near the island of Crete. Recognizing the danger, Paul, drawing from both divine insight and practical experience, warned the crew and passengers that continuing the journey could result in disaster, with potential loss of the ship, cargo, and lives (Acts 27:9-10). However, his advice was overruled by the centurion, who was persuaded by the ship's captain and owner to press on (Acts 27:11). This decision set the stage for the dire circumstances that would soon follow, as the crew's disregard for Paul's warning would lead them into a severe storm.

The Storm at Sea: Divine Assurance Amidst Despair (Acts 27:21-26)

As they sailed further, they encountered a massive storm, described as a "Northeaster" (Euraquilo), which swept down from the island and caught the ship, driving it uncontrollably across the sea (Acts 27:14-15). The storm raged for many days, blotting out the sun and stars, and the crew, unable to navigate, lost all hope of survival (Acts 27:20). It was in this moment of despair that Paul emerged as a beacon of hope. After days of silence, Paul stood before the crew and passengers, offering them a message of divine assurance. He recounted how an angel of God had appeared to him, reassuring him that he and all those aboard would be spared, though the ship would be lost. Paul's words, "Keep up your courage, men, for I have faith in God that it will happen just as he told me" (Acts 27:25), highlight his unwavering trust in God's promises and his role as a spiritual leader, even in the most desperate circumstances.

Shipwreck on Malta: God's Protection in the Midst of Disaster (Acts 27:27-44)

After two weeks adrift, the crew sensed that they were approaching land, and under Paul's guidance, they took soundings and confirmed the depth was decreasing, indicating land was near (Acts 27:27-28). As daylight approached, they sighted a bay with a sandy beach and decided to run the ship aground there. However, the ship struck a sandbar before reaching the shore, causing it to break apart under the force of the waves (Acts 27:41). In the ensuing chaos, the soldiers planned to kill the prisoners to prevent any from escaping, but Julius, wanting to spare Paul's life, intervened and ordered those who could swim to jump overboard first and get to land. Remarkably, as Paul had promised, all 276 passengers and crew made it safely to shore, fulfilling the divine assurance given to Paul (Acts 27:44). This miraculous preservation of life amidst such a catastrophic shipwreck underscores God's providence and the fulfillment of His promises.

Hospitality on Malta: A Season of Ministry and Miracles (Acts 28:1-10)

Once ashore, the survivors discovered they were on the island of Malta. The islanders, described as unusually kind, welcomed them and provided for their needs. During this time, Paul continued his ministry, even while recovering from the shipwreck. When Paul was bitten by a viper and suffered no harm, the islanders initially thought he was a god, but Paul's focus remained on directing their attention to the true God (Acts 28:3-6). His ministry extended to healing the father of Publius, the chief official of the island, who was suffering from fever and dysentery. This miracle, along with others, led to widespread healing on the island and solidified Paul's reputation as a man of God (Acts 28:8-9). Paul's time on Malta, therefore, became a season of fruitful ministry, marked by God's miraculous interventions and the spread of the Gospel to yet another part of the Roman world.

Arrival in Rome: The Fulfillment of God's Purpose (Acts 28:11-16)

After three months on Malta, Paul and his companions secured passage on another ship and finally completed their journey to Rome. Upon arrival, Paul was allowed to live by himself, under house arrest, with a soldier to guard him (Acts 28:16). This arrangement, while restrictive, also provided Paul with the freedom to receive visitors and continue his ministry. For the next two years, Paul preached the kingdom of God and taught about the Lord Jesus Christ "with all boldness and without hindrance" (Acts 28:30-31). Paul's arrival in Rome marked the fulfillment of God's plan for him to testify about Christ in the capital of the Roman

Empire, just as the Lord had promised him in a vision earlier in his journey (Acts 23:11).

Reflections on Paul's Voyage to Rome

Paul's journey to Rome serves as a profound testament to God's sovereignty, protection, and faithfulness. Despite the numerous dangers, including a life-threatening storm and shipwreck, Paul remained steadfast in his mission, fully trusting in God's promises. His ability to inspire hope and courage in others, even in the face of overwhelming odds, reflects his deep faith and his understanding that his life was in God's hands.

Moreover, Paul's experience illustrates how God can use seemingly dire circumstances to further His purposes. What began as a perilous journey to stand trial in Rome became an opportunity for Paul to spread the Gospel to new regions, including Malta, and to bear witness in the heart of the Roman Empire. Paul's time in Rome, though spent under house arrest, was marked by significant ministry, as he continued to teach and preach, influencing both Jews and Gentiles alike.

In the broader narrative of Acts, Paul's journey to Rome is not just a personal story of endurance and faith; it represents the unstoppable advance of the Gospel. Despite opposition, natural disasters, and human schemes, the message of Christ continued to spread, reaching even the most powerful city in the ancient world. Paul's voyage to Rome, therefore, stands as a powerful reminder that God's purposes will prevail, and His word will go forth, even in the face of adversity.

This journey, marked by Paul's resilience, divine encounters, and the enduring power of the Gospel, continues to inspire Christians today, reminding us that in every storm and trial, God's presence is with us, guiding, protecting, and fulfilling His purposes in our lives.

CHAPTER 14

FINAL IMPRISONMENT AND MARTYRDOM

The Final Days of the Apostle Paul: A Legacy of Faith and Martyrdom

The final days of the Apostle Paul, as recorded in early Christian tradition and supported by historical accounts, are a solemn and powerful chapter in the history of the early Church. These days reflect the culmination of a life devoted to the service of Christ, marked by profound theological contributions, relentless missionary work, and an unwavering commitment to the Gospel, even unto death.

Final Imprisonment in Rome

Paul's final imprisonment is traditionally believed to have taken place in Rome, where he was likely held under house arrest, as he had been during his first Roman imprisonment. However, unlike his earlier confinement, which is documented in the Book of Acts, the New Testament provides few details about this final period of imprisonment. Some early Christian writings and historical sources, however, offer glimpses into what transpired during this time.

The Writing of 2 Timothy: During this period, Paul is believed to have written his final letter, 2 Timothy, which serves as a poignant and personal farewell to his close associate and spiritual son, Timothy. In this letter, Paul expresses a clear awareness of his impending martyrdom, stating, "For I am already being poured out as a drink offering, and the time of my departure has come" (2 Timothy 4:6). He reflects on his life's work with the famous words, "I have fought the good fight, I have finished the race, I have kept the faith" (2 Timothy 4:7). Paul's tone is one of solemn resignation, yet also of victorious assurance in the eternal reward that awaits him. He urges Timothy to visit him in Rome before winter (2 Timothy 4:9, 21), indicating his deep desire for companionship during what he senses are his final days. This letter is rich with theological reflection, pastoral advice, and personal requests, revealing Paul's deep concern for the future of the Church and the well-being of his fellow workers in the Gospel.

The Conditions of Imprisonment: While the New Testament does not detail the conditions of Paul's final imprisonment, early Christian writings suggest that it was a harsher and more isolated experience compared to his earlier house arrest. Unlike his previous imprisonment, during which Paul had considerable freedom to receive visitors and continue his ministry, his final confinement is thought to have been more restrictive. Some traditions suggest that Paul was held in the Mamertine Prison, a grim and dank dungeon in Rome, where prisoners were often kept before execution. Despite these harsh conditions, Paul remained steadfast in his faith, using his final days to continue writing and encouraging the Christian communities.

The Martyrdom of Paul

The exact details surrounding Paul's martyrdom are not comprehensively documented, but early Christian tradition provides significant insights. According to accounts by early Church Fathers such as Clement of Rome, Ignatius of Antioch, and Tertullian, Paul was martyred in Rome during the reign of Emperor Nero, who initiated a brutal persecution of Christians following the Great Fire of Rome in AD 64.

Execution by Beheading: Tradition holds that Paul was executed by beheading, a method of execution reserved for Roman citizens, as it was considered a quicker and less painful death compared to crucifixion. This event is believed to have occurred outside the city walls of Rome, near the site now commemorated by the Basilica of St. Paul Outside the Walls. The choice of beheading, as opposed to crucifixion, underscores Paul's status as a Roman citizen and reflects the legal privileges that accompanied this status, even in death.

Significance of Martyrdom: Paul's martyrdom is viewed by early Christians and subsequent generations as the ultimate testimony to his unwavering faith in Christ. His willingness to face death rather than renounce his faith served as a powerful example to the early Church, inspiring countless believers to remain steadfast in the face of persecution. Paul's death, like his life, was a reflection of his profound commitment to the Gospel, and it solidified his role as one of the most significant figures in Christian history.

Paul's Enduring Legacy

Paul's legacy extends far beyond his martyrdom. As a missionary, theologian, and writer, Paul's influence on Christian theology and practice is unparalleled. His letters, which make up a significant portion of the New Testament, offer deep insights into the nature of salvation, the role of the Church, and the transformative power of the Gospel.

Theological Contributions: Paul's letters are foundational to Christian theology. His teachings on justification by faith, the nature of the Church as the body of Christ, and the work of the Holy Spirit have shaped Christian doctrine for centuries. Paul's ability to articulate the complexities of the Christian faith in ways that were both theologically profound and practically applicable has made his writings enduring sources of guidance and reflection for believers across all denominations.

Inspiration for Christian Living: Throughout history, Paul's life and writings have inspired countless Christians to live lives of faith, perseverance, and commitment to the Gospel. His example of enduring suffering for the sake of Christ, his tireless efforts to spread the Gospel to Jews and Gentiles alike, and his profound understanding of God's redemptive plan have left an indelible mark on the Church. Paul's teachings continue to resonate with believers, offering a blueprint for Christian living that emphasizes faith, love, and obedience to God's will.

Influence on Christian Thought and Scholarship: Paul's writings have been the subject of extensive study and commentary by theologians, scholars, and clergy throughout the history of the Church. His epistles are central to the development of Christian doctrine and have been pivotal in major theological debates, from the early Church councils to the Reformation and beyond. Paul's ability to address complex theological issues with clarity and depth has made his letters enduring texts for study, interpretation, and application in the life of the Church.

The final days of the Apostle Paul, while shrouded in some historical uncertainty, represent the culmination of a life lived in full devotion to Christ. His final imprisonment, his writings during this time, and his eventual martyrdom in Rome serve as a powerful testament to his faith, resilience, and the impact of his ministry. Paul's legacy as an apostle, missionary, theologian, and martyr continues to influence and inspire Christians around the world. His writings remain a vital part of Christian scripture, offering timeless truths about the nature of God, the power of the Gospel, and the call to live a life of faithfulness to Christ, even in the face of adversity.

CHAPTER 15

LEGACY AND INFLUENCE

Examining the Enduring Impact of the Apostle Paul on Christianity

The Apostle Paul's legacy within Christianity is unparalleled, leaving an indelible mark on the faith through his pioneering missionary work, profound theological insights, and timeless writings. His contributions continue to shape Christian theology, practice, and the global understanding of the Gospel.

1. Pioneering Missionary Work: Expanding the Gospel's Reach

Paul's missionary journeys, meticulously recorded in the Book of Acts, were foundational in spreading Christianity across the Roman Empire. Paul was not merely a traveler; he was a relentless evangelist who brought the Gospel to both Jewish and Gentile territories, establishing and nurturing Christian communities in cities like Corinth, Ephesus, Philippi, and Thessalonica. His unwavering commitment to preaching Christ crucified (1 Corinthians 1:23) in diverse cultural settings broke down the barriers between Jews and Gentiles, making Christianity a universal faith rather than a sect of Judaism. Paul's role as the "Apostle to the Gentiles" (Romans 11:13) was instrumental in expanding the reach of Christianity far beyond its origins in Judea, laying the groundwork for the faith to become a global religion.

2. Theological Depth: Shaping Christian Doctrine

Paul's letters, which constitute a significant portion of the New Testament, are rich in theological content and have profoundly influenced Christian thought for centuries. His epistles address essential doctrines such as justification by faith (Romans 3:28), salvation by grace (Ephesians 2:8-9), and the role of the Law in the life of believers (Galatians 3:24-25). Paul's teachings on the nature of the Church as the "body of Christ" (1 Corinthians 12:12-27) provide a framework for understanding the unity and diversity within the Christian community. Additionally, his exposition on the resurrection of the dead (1 Corinthians 15) offers a foundational understanding of Christian eschatology. These teachings continue to be central to Christian theology, with his letter to the Romans often considered the most systematic presentation of Christian doctrine in the New Testament.

3. Emphasis on Grace: The Heart of the Gospel
One of Paul's most significant contributions to Christian theology is his emphasis on God's grace as the means of salvation. Paul repeatedly underscores that salvation is a gift from God, received through faith, and not earned by works (Romans 11:6). This doctrine of justification by faith alone became a cornerstone of the Protestant Reformation and remains central to many Christian denominations today. His articulation of grace in letters like Ephesians and Galatians continues to shape Christian soteriology, offering believers assurance that their salvation is secured by God's unmerited favor rather than human effort. Paul's understanding of grace has not only influenced theological discussions but has also provided comfort and hope to countless Christians throughout history.

4. Ethical Guidance: Principles for Christian Living
Paul's letters go beyond theological instruction to offer practical guidance for Christian living. His teachings on love (1 Corinthians 13), unity (Philippians 2:1-4), and the ethical

implications of the Gospel are enduring guides for believers. Paul's exhortations to "walk in a manner worthy of the calling" (Ephesians 4:1) emphasize the transformative power of the Gospel in everyday life. His instructions on moral conduct, community relationships, and social responsibilities provide a framework for ethical living that has shaped Christian behavior for millennia. Paul's teachings remain relevant today, offering wisdom on how to live out the Christian faith in a complex and often challenging world.

5. Influence on Christian Leadership: Establishing Church Order

Paul's pastoral epistles—1 Timothy, 2 Timothy, and Titus—are crucial texts for understanding the organization and leadership of the early Church. In these letters, Paul outlines the qualifications for elders and deacons (1 Timothy 3:1-13; Titus 1:5-9), emphasizing the importance of moral integrity, doctrinal soundness, and pastoral care. He provides guidance on managing church affairs, addressing false teachings, and fostering a healthy community. These letters have had a lasting impact on the structure and leadership of Christian churches, influencing how leaders are selected and how churches are governed. Paul's pastoral wisdom continues to guide church leaders in their responsibilities and challenges, ensuring that the Church remains faithful to its mission.

6. Theological Diversity: Engaging Early Christian Thought

While Paul's writings form a substantial part of the New Testament, they also reflect the theological diversity of early Christianity. His interactions with other apostles, such as Peter and James, and his correspondence with various Christian communities, reveal the dynamic nature of theological discussions and the development of doctrine in the early Church. Paul's letters often address specific issues and controversies, such as the role of the Law for Gentile converts (Galatians 2:11-14), showing his engagement with differing perspectives within the Christian movement. This diversity is a testament to the richness of early Christian thought and the process by which key doctrines were articulated and affirmed. Paul's ability to navigate these complexities and offer coherent theological responses has contributed significantly to the development of Christian doctrine.

7. Literary Excellence: Rhetorical Mastery and Persuasive Power

Paul's letters are not only theologically profound but also exhibit a high level of rhetorical skill and literary excellence. His use of rhetorical devices, such as diatribe (Romans 3:1-9), metaphor (1 Corinthians 9:24-27), and typology (Romans 5:12-21), demonstrates his ability to communicate complex ideas in ways that are both persuasive and memorable. Paul's letters have been admired for their clarity, logical structure, and emotional depth, making them enduring classics in Christian literature. His ability to address diverse audiences—from the philosophical Greeks in Athens (Acts 17:22-34) to the devout Jews in Jerusalem—highlights his versatility as a communicator and his deep understanding of the cultural contexts in which he ministered.

The legacy and influence of the Apostle Paul within Christianity are immeasurable. His pioneering missionary work, profound theological insights, emphasis on grace, and practical ethical guidance have shaped the foundation of Christian faith and practice. Paul's writings continue to be a cornerstone of Christian theology, offering timeless truths that guide believers in their understanding of God, salvation, and the Christian life. His contributions have inspired generations of Christians and continue to resonate with believers around the world, illustrating the enduring impact of one man's dedication to spreading the Gospel of Jesus Christ. Through his life, teachings, and letters, Paul remains a pivotal figure in the history of Christianity, whose influence will continue to be felt for centuries to come.

CONCLUSION

The Life and Contributions of the Apostle Paul: A Pillar of Christian History

The Apostle Paul stands as one of the most towering figures in the history of Christianity. His transformation from a zealous persecutor of Christians to a devoted apostle and theologian underscores the profound impact of encountering Christ. Paul's enduring influence on the Christian faith is vast and multifaceted, leaving an indelible mark on theology, mission, and pastoral care. His life and works continue to inspire and guide believers across generations.

Missionary Zeal: Expanding the Reach of Christianity

Paul's missionary journeys, as chronicled in the Book of Acts, were instrumental in the expansion of Christianity beyond its Jewish roots. His tireless efforts took the Gospel to the Gentile world, establishing Christian communities throughout the Roman Empire, including in major cities such as Corinth, Ephesus, and Philippi. Paul's commitment to preaching the Gospel, often at great personal risk, laid the foundation for the growth of Christianity as a global faith. His declaration, "I have become all things to all people so that by all possible means I might save some" (1 Corinthians 9:22), exemplifies his dedication to reaching diverse audiences. Modern missionaries continue to draw inspiration from Paul's zeal, adaptability, and strategic approach to evangelism.

Theological Depth: Shaping Christian Doctrine

Paul's letters, which make up a significant portion of the New Testament, delve deeply into essential theological concepts that have shaped Christian doctrine for centuries. His writings explore profound themes such as grace (Ephesians 2:8-9), faith (Romans 5:1), justification (Romans 3:28), and the role of the Law in the life of believers (Galatians 3:23-25). Paul's epistles, particularly Romans and Galatians, provide a systematic presentation of Christian theology, addressing the nature of sin, salvation, and the transformative power of the Gospel. His insights into the relationship between the Law and grace have had a lasting impact on Christian theology, influencing key theological developments throughout history, including the Protestant Reformation.

Emphasis on Grace: The Cornerstone of Christian Salvation

Paul's emphasis on God's grace as the means of salvation is one of his most significant contributions to Christian theology. In his writings, particularly in the Letter to the Romans, Paul articulates that salvation is not earned by works but is a gift from God, received through faith in Jesus Christ (Romans 3:24-25). This doctrine of justification by faith became a cornerstone of Christian belief, particularly during the Reformation, when it was championed by figures like Martin Luther. Paul's teachings on grace continue to shape Christian understanding of salvation, providing assurance to believers that their standing before God is based on His mercy, not human merit.

Ethical Guidance: Practical Teachings for Christian Living

Paul's letters are rich in ethical guidance, offering practical instructions on how Christians should live out their faith. His teachings on love (1 Corinthians 13), unity (Ephesians 4:3-6), and the ethical implications of the Gospel (Romans 12:1-2) remain foundational for Christian moral and spiritual life. Paul's exhortations to "live by the Spirit" (Galatians 5:16) and to "put on the new self" (Ephesians 4:24) encourage believers to embody the transformative power of the Gospel in their daily lives. His emphasis on love as the greatest of all virtues (1 Corinthians 13:13) continues to guide Christian interactions and community life.

Pastoral Care: Foundational Guidance for Church Leadership

Paul's pastoral epistles—1 Timothy, 2 Timothy, and Titus—provide critical guidance for church leadership and structure. In these letters, Paul outlines the qualifications for elders and deacons (1 Timothy 3:1-13; Titus 1:5-9), emphasizing the importance of moral integrity, doctrinal soundness, and the ability to teach and shepherd the congregation. These epistles also address the need for sound doctrine and the pastoral care of the Christian community, warning against false teachings and encouraging the nurturing of the flock. Paul's instructions in these letters have been foundational for the organization and governance of Christian churches, influencing how leaders are chosen and how church communities are nurtured and protected.

Literary Excellence: Rhetorical Skill and Persuasive Power

Paul's letters are not only theologically profound but also exhibit a high degree of rhetorical skill and literary excellence. His ability to craft persuasive arguments, employ rhetorical questions (Romans 6:1-2), and use vivid metaphors (2 Timothy 4:7) demonstrates his mastery of language and his effectiveness as a communicator. Paul's epistles have been celebrated for their clarity, logical structure, and emotional depth, making them timeless classics in Christian literature. His writings continue to be studied for their literary qualities as well as their theological content, serving as models of effective communication of the Gospel.

Legacy of Perseverance: An Example of Faith in Adversity

Paul's life is a testament to perseverance in the face of adversity. Despite facing numerous hardships—including imprisonment, beatings, shipwrecks, and constant threats to his life—Paul remained steadfast in his mission to spread the Gospel. His declaration, "I can do all this through him who gives me strength" (Philippians 4:13), reflects his unwavering reliance on Christ. Paul's endurance, even unto martyrdom, serves as a powerful example for Christians facing challenges today. His life encourages believers to remain faithful and committed to Christ, regardless of the trials they may encounter.

The life and contributions of the Apostle Paul are foundational to the Christian faith. His missionary zeal, theological depth, emphasis on grace, ethical guidance, and pastoral care have shaped the beliefs, practices, and understanding of the Gospel for Christians throughout history. Paul's writings continue to serve as a source of inspiration, guidance, and theological reflection for believers around the world. His legacy as a missionary, theologian, and pastor underscores the transformative power of encountering Christ and the enduring impact of a life dedicated to spreading the Good News. Paul's influence on Christianity is profound and far-reaching, ensuring that his contributions will continue to resonate through the ages.